# Life in the USA

*An Immigrant's Guide to
Understanding Americans*

Planaria J. Price
Euphronia Awakuni

Ann Arbor
The University of Michigan Press

# Dedication

To all of our wonderful students at Evans Community Adult School and Glendale Community College, past, present, and future: with deep appreciation for sharing their questions, confusion, and embarrassing experiences in this new land with us.

# Acknowledgments

This book was the vision of Kelly Sippell, our incredibly gifted and understanding editor at the University of Michigan Press. We, and our students, thank her for stimulating us to put all of their questions and embarrassing experiences in print so that others can better understand the American culture.

# Contents

# Introduction

Welcome to the USA!

You must be both excited and nervous to be here in this country of more than 300 million people. Try to remember that you will probably find that America and Americans are very different from your own culture and country. Your first few days and experiences in America will not be very similar to what you have seen in movies from Hollywood or in American television programs.

We have taught ESL to adults in the Los Angeles, California area—in a large public adult school in Los Angeles and in a small community college in Glendale, California—for many years. We have met students from more than 96 countries. This book is a collection of letters our students have written to us with their questions about American culture. They share the experiences that have confused them.

The book has nine sections. First, you will read the letters our students wrote (we fixed the grammar and the spelling). Then you will read our answers. Often, when Americans write letters, they add the words P.S. at the bottom. P.S. means that extra information and facts are added to the letter. At the end of each section of letters, we have added a P.S. to show you the most important things to remember. We also have added a few cautions—things to be careful of.

We hope that these questions and answers will help you feel better about being in the United States of America. We hope that we can save you from having some of the embarrassing and confusing situations that our students experienced.

Because you are probably not fluent in English, we have tried to make the vocabulary and grammar as simple as possible. Most of the language is at an intermediate language level. When we have used a word that you might not know, we have explained it.

Understanding America and Americans (in this book, *America* and *Americans* refer primarily to the United States of America and the people who were born here) will take you a long time. (Yes, others not born here are Americans too, but they are **usually** not part of the **general** descriptions included in this book.) The students who wrote letters for this book and we, the authors, hope that you will enjoy this book and that it will make your experience in the United States more comfortable.

## Important!

Please understand that this book includes **general statements** about Americans. The United States of America is a large country made up of many different groups of people whose families have come from all over the world. You will find many differences from what we say, depending on whom you meet and where you live. We have tried to be as accurate as possible in describing the accepted customs of the **average American** from New York to Los Angeles, from Florida to Washington State, and from Hawaii and Alaska. (The authors live in a big city on the West Coast, but the publisher and editor is in the Midwest, and we encountered many areas in which we did not agree on what "Americans" do or think.)

## Helpful Hints

Use your eyes! Look at American newspaper comics. Read children's books and newspaper advice columns. Watch television dramas, comedies, and movies. All of this will give you more information about general American culture.

The letters and their answers will help you understand parts of American culture. But even if you read the whole book, you will still have questions and may not understand why Americans do the things they do. The best way for you to learn about Americans—what is considered common, what is considered polite or rude (not polite), what is good or bad, and why Americans do what they do and in which situations—is to pay attention to what happens around you. Ask yourself, "Would this be common in my culture?" "Is it OK here? Why?" "What is the situation?" A helpful reference list of 101 Characteristics of Americans/American Culture can be found at www.press.umich.edu/esl/.

## Television

For some people, the easiest and most comfortable way to observe American culture is to watch television. Situation comedies are especially helpful. These programs have the same characters every week, and each week something different and funny happens to them. Popular programs like "Friends," or "Everybody Loves Raymond" are good examples to help you understand some American values. Be careful! Be sure to ask an American if the programs you are watching show *typical* American culture. Programs like "Married with Children," "South Park," "The Simpsons," daytime soap operas (dramas or stories), and many talk shows and reality shows have situations in which the people are often very rude and not normal. Americans like those programs because they show the opposite of what the average American considers polite and acceptable. (Some daytime dramas, however, can be good for improving language because they repeat language day to day to help viewers follow the story.)

Some programs will help you understand American law and values: what is considered right and what is considered wrong. TV shows like "Judge Judy" or "The People's Court" are examples.

Because television shows change all the time, be sure to ask an American friend or teacher his or her opinions about a particular program. Ask if it shows **typical** American life. You can also ask someone you don't know! As you will discover in this book, most Americans are friendly, and sometimes even strangers will tell you their opinions. Do not feel afraid to ask.

### Newspaper Comics

The cartoons and comics in a newspaper are great ways to learn about typical American cultural values. In America, newspaper comics are written for the enjoyment of the educated American adult. Sometimes they are easier to learn from than television because they don't move! You can look at a comic for a long time to help you understand the picture and the words. Find one or two that you like, and read those all the time. Comics are not easy to understand, but little by little, you will start to be familiar with the characters and their relationships to each other. Be sure to look at the pictures very carefully to learn about American body language. Understand that the words in the cartoon balloons (the words above the characters' heads) are written to sound like conversation, so the spelling and grammar will seem strange. For example: *I hafta go* means "I have to go." *Doncha wanna* means "don't you want to." *He's gonna do it* means "he is going to do it."

### Newspaper Advice Columns

The advice columns in a newspaper are good sources to help you learn what is considered polite in American culture. The most common ones in newspapers are "Ask Abby," "Ask Amy," or "Ask Carolyn." Also try a free website called www.dearmrsweb.com. Of course, when you first start reading advice columns, the English in these columns will not be easy for you to understand. The writers use a lot of idioms and slang (informal language) that you might not yet know. Read advice columns every day and, slowly, you will get a very clear idea of what is considered common and polite in American culture.

## Libraries and Books

Public libraries in the United States are free and open to everyone. You need some sort of identification to get a library card, and then you can check out books, CDs, videos, or DVDs. You can use computers at the library for free. Check with your local library to see what is available. In the library, go to the children's book section, and check out (borrow) the classic American children's books (ask the librarian to recommend some). Try reading American folk stories ("grandmother stories") and American history. In all cultures, children's stories provide the foundation of the cultural values, vocabulary, and grammar of the people. Your grandmother's stories taught you your language and values. The American stories will do the same for the English language and American cultural values.

## Music

If you need to improve your English, listen to American popular music of the past 40 years. Our students recommend Frank Sinatra, Nat King Cole, Elvis Presley, the Beatles, the Rolling Stones, the Doors, U2, and Celine Dion. Singers like these sing clearly, and listening to that music will help you exercise your listening skills and increase your knowledge of American culture.

## Success!

You will find that by watching television and movies, by reading comics and advice columns and classic children's stories, and by listening to American pop songs, your English will improve and you will find that you understand better why Americans do what they do.

## P.S.

### Using Websites

For more detailed information on subjects covered in this book, we recommend that you:

✓ Do a Google search (www.google.com) by just typing in the name of the subject you are interested in.

✓ Go to www.wikipedia.org, and type in the name of the subject you are interested in.

✓ Visit http://shagtown.com/days to learn about American holidays.

✓ Go to www.census.gov for accurate but sometimes confusing statistics about the United States.

✓ Get quick facts from the U.S. Census by trying: http://quickfacts.census.gov or www.factfinder.census.gov.

For more detailed information, try:

✓ www.infoplease.com or www.factmonster.com.

**Caution**

You can find thousands of websites with information about the subjects in this book, but be careful. Not all the information found on the different sites is true, and not all websites agree. Always be careful with your sources, and don't trust just one website or one person's opinion.

# First Impressions

# A. America's Size and Its People

*Teacher:*
*All my life I wanted to come to America. It was the land of my dreams. But, Teacher, I have been here two months, and this is not what I thought I would see at all. I thought I would see only white people speaking perfect English, like in the movies. I thought everyone was tall and thin with big blue eyes and blonde hair. But everywhere I go, I see Latinos and Asians and blacks, and yesterday I saw some people wearing their own national clothes. Also not all the signs are in English, Teacher. They're in Spanish and Chinese and Korean and Armenian, and even my language. I hear people speaking so many different languages. Will I ever meet an American and learn English?*

*Phan*

---

Dear Phan,

First of all, you probably are seeing a lot of Americans. Because America is a land of immigrants, the people you see have ancestors (generations of grandparents) who came from some other country. In fact, almost every country in the world is represented by the Americans you see every day. The people might have the same coloring, eyes, hair, etc., of their ancestors, but most of their families have been here for many generations and are Americans. Those who are speaking in their languages are probably new immigrants. You see a lot of signs in different languages to help the new immigrants, like you, who have not yet learned English well.

*Dear Teacher,*

*Every day on my way to school I see people lying on the streets, and sometimes the Americans stop and talk to them and even give them money. In my country, the homeless rob or kill you. Most of the city I see here is clean, but some areas are very dirty with ugly writing on the buildings. If my grandmother were here she would want to die. Teacher, I do not mean to be disrespectful, but this is not the America I expected. Is this normal?*

*Sokphally*

---

Sokphally,

I know that you didn't expect to find so many unpleasant things here in America. It must be quite a surprise for you. Let me explain some of the reasons. What you saw in Hollywood movies often showed an unreal America. What you are seeing now is a part of the real America.

Homelessness breaks my heart. There are just too many homeless people in this country. More than 20 percent of them are sick in some way and need help; others take drugs or drink too much alcohol. Some people lose their jobs, and then, because they do not have money to pay for their homes, they lose them. The U.S. cities with warm weather have more homeless people. I often give food or money to those who look sick or disabled. I stay away from anyone who looks dangerous, but most homeless are harmless. They make me feel sad for them and very fortunate for what I have.

The dirty streets also make me sad. Most U.S. cities do not use street cleaners like in your country, so there is no one to take away the trash on the sidewalks. Each person must be responsible for his or her own garbage. Too often, people are lazy and selfish. Throwing trash on the ground is called *littering*, and it is against the law. Actually, if you throw trash on the highway, you could be required to pay as much as $1,000. This is an example of something that is confusing about America. You have the freedom to choose what you want to do to make yourself happy, but your freedom cannot take away anyone else's freedom. So if someone is happy throwing garbage and that makes me unhappy, he or she has to stop because the law will protect me.

The writing on the buildings is called *graffiti*. It is against the law. If you are caught, you will go to jail or have to pay money. When people use their freedom to write all over someone else's property, buildings, and walls, they are taking away our rights and freedom to enjoy the beauty of what we see.

You asked me if all of this is common, and I have to say that it is. But that doesn't mean that all Americans like it.

---

*Teacher:*

*It took me 3 hours to fly from my country to America. Then it took me 5½ hours to fly from Florida to California! This is an enormous country! The buildings are so tall. The cars look like trucks. And, Teacher, excuse me, but the people are big too! I have never seen so many fat people in my life! And, Teacher, why do people keep backing away from me when I talk to them? Is all of this normal?*

*Juan José*

---

Dear Juan José,

Yes, I think this is common in most of the cities. America is a very big country. It is the third largest country in the world. The main

4

part measures 3,718,711 square miles. When you add the 6,470 square miles of the 132 Hawaiian Islands and the 591,004 square miles of Alaska, you get a country of 4,316,185 square miles. That is BIG!

Unfortunately, many Americans (some sources say 66 percent) are overweight. This is a sensitive topic for Americans, Juan José. There are many American lifestyle factors that lead to extra weight. Also, many Americans are very serious about exercising every day.

Many Americans like to have open spaces around them. This comes from a time in American history when there was a lot of empty land. Some Americans like to drive big cars. You may notice how much space and distance Americans seem to want from other people. Americans like a little area of space all around them. This is called *elbow room*. Put your hands on your hips, and turn around in

a circle. This is about the amount of "personal space that Americans like." When an American seems to back away from you, it is not because he or she doesn't like you. If you stand close (as you might in your culture), Americans get nervous because you are in their personal space.

---

*Dear Teacher,*

*Many young people have writing all over their bodies and big rings in their ears and noses and other places. They have purple hair, and their pants are falling off, showing their underwear. Their stomachs show too. My father would kill me if I looked like that. It is so ugly.*

*Jasper*

---

Jasper,

A lot of the teenagers look strange to me, too. Young people, in all cultures, want to be independent from their parents, and because independence is so admired and encouraged in America, many teenagers are allowed to dress to look different. Some of them even want to scare the older people by their differences. What you are seeing on the streets is current fashion across the whole United States. Fashions come and go. At this time, the fashion is to decorate the skin with tattoos, to put lots of rings in the body, and to have different colors of hair. Today, many parents and grandparents of young children are hoping that this particular fashion will change by the time their American children become teenagers!

---

# P.S.

- ✓ America is the third largest country in the world.
- ✓ America has a population of more than 300,000,000 people.
- ✓ 66 percent of Americans are overweight.
- ✓ Americans like their personal space.
- ✓ Americans come in all colors, have all types of religions, and speak many languages from all over the world.
- ✓ Approximately 1 percent of Americans are homeless (3.5 million people).
- ✓ About 39 percent of the homeless are children.
- ✓ About 40 percent of the homeless are people who fought in wars for the United States.
- ✓ The streets of major cities are often dirty.
- ✓ Teenagers wear clothes that look funny, and many teenagers have tattoos and body piercings.

## Caution

- ✓ Be careful with strangers and use good judgment!
- ✓ Littering (throwing garbage on the streets) is against the law.
- ✓ Be sure not to come too close to Americans when you talk to them. Respect their personal space.
- ✓ Graffiti and tagging (writing on walls and streets) is against the law.
- ✓ Loitering (standing around in public and doing nothing) is against the law.

# B. A Brief History of the USA

*Teacher,*

*You keep saying that we cannot learn a language without learning the culture and that we need to know the history to understand the culture. I am reading some of the children's story books you recommended, and I am trying to watch the History Channel as much as possible. But, Teacher, why can't I smoke anywhere anymore? Why do you want me to call you by your first name and not "Teacher"?*

*Dara*

----

Dara,

It's great that you are reading the books and watching television. Remember that learning a new language can take eight to ten years! You cannot possibly understand everything at once, but slowly the pieces of the puzzle will fall into place.

It might help you to know that America, as we know it, really began in 1620 when people—called the Pilgrims—came to the eastern coast of America as immigrants from England. They wanted to be free to practice their religion. At that time, a lot of what is now the USA was owned by the King of England. He allowed the Pilgrims to establish a colony (a small piece of land for England) in what is now the state of Massachusetts. Soon after the Pilgrims arrived, others came from other parts of England and Western Europe. They also wanted to be free to practice religion; what they really wanted was a *freedom of choice.* They wanted to make their own place in society based on who they were and not who their parents were. (In many European countries, those with royal blood controlled

8

everything.) They wanted freedom to choose their own futures. They did not want to be told what to do by their government, church, or families. Over the past 400 years, immigrants from almost all countries in the world have come to America for many of the same reasons. You probably did, too.

In 1776, there were 13 colonies, and the people wanted to have complete freedom from the King of England and the British laws. They fought a war for their independence from England, and they won that war. A few years later, the United States of America was officially formed. The Constitution forming the new government said that the people had the right to certain freedoms and that the laws of the government would protect those rights.

Then in the early 1800s, if the new Americans were not happy with their lives, they would leave their families and move west where there was a lot of land. These people were called pioneers. As you know, this country is so big, and the pioneers felt that they could build homes anywhere they wanted and the land was theirs. They had farms and were extremely independent. As long as the pioneers followed the laws, they could do whatever they wanted. But some of the laws were not good or fair. The Native Americans, whose land was taken by the new Americans, and the African Americans, who had been kidnapped from Africa and forced to come to America as slaves, also had the same dream of having freedom and independence.

In the 21st century, people who live in America know that they have the right to live their own lives and to pursue their own happiness. In 2008, Americans elected the first African-American president, proving that Americans do believe in giving opportunity to all. But it does get complicated. To be sure that one person's freedom will not take away another person's freedom, America tries to follow the *rule of law,* and the laws try to equally protect the rights of everyone. That's why you can't smoke in my class or a restaurant because your happiness in smoking might take away my happiness in breathing fresh air.

You will find that it doesn't matter what color someone's skin, eyes, or hair is—the majority of the people living in America want to be free to make their own decisions about their own lives. Because of the idea expressed in the Declaration of Independence that everyone is equal, Americans are informal. As you have noticed, Americans often speak to anyone, no matter the age, gender, profession, or situation. This is why I ask you to call me by my first name even though I am your teacher and older. To me, we are equals.

## P.S.

- ✓ Americans believe in freedom of choice.
- ✓ Americans are individualistic and like to be able to pursue their own interests and desires as long as it doesn't harm anyone else.
- ✓ America follows the rule of law.

# C. The Melting Pot of America: Statistics on Where People Come From and Their Languages

## 1. Race/Ethnicity

White 75%

Hispanic or Latino (of any race) 14.50%

African American 12%

Asian 4%

Native American and Alaskan Native 0.9%

Native Hawaiian and Pacific Islander 0.1%

Other/Multiracial 6%

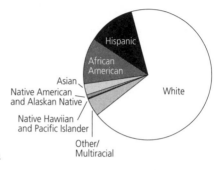

Source: U.S. Census 2000.

*Note:* These numbers add up to more than 100 percent because many people claim two or more races or ethnicities.

## 2. Languages (U.S. Census statistics from 2000)

Approximately 337 languages are spoken (or signed) in homes in the USA. Many (176) of those languages are spoken by the Native Peoples of America. Of the population of the USA, 92 percent of the people say that they speak English "well" or "very well."

| | |
|---|---|
| English | 214.8 million<br>82% (over the age of 5) speak<br>only English at home |
| Spanish (including Creole) | 28 million |
| Chinese | 2.0 million |
| French (including Creole) | 1.6 million |
| German | 1.4 million |
| Tagalog | 1.2 million |
| Vietnamese | 1.1 million |

The other main languages spoken by people in their homes are (from most to least number of speakers): Italian, Korean, Russian, Polish, Arabic, Portuguese, Japanese, Greek, Hindi, Persian, Urdu, Gujarati, Armenian, Hebrew, Cambodian, Yiddish, Navajo, Hmong, and Yoruba.

## 3. Religions

Because the laws of the United States guarantee complete separation of the government and religion, the U.S. Census (information gathered every 10 years) does not ask for people's religion. These statistics come from various private surveys and are estimates based on the 2000 Census.

| | |
|---|---|
| Christianity | 76.7% |
| Protestantism | 52.0% |
| Roman Catholicism | 24.7% |
| Agnostic, atheist, no religion | 14.2% |
| Other religions | 6.0% |
| Judaism | 1.4% |
| Islam | 0.5% |
| Buddhism | 0.5% |
| Hinduism | 0.4% |
| Unitarian Universalism | 0.3% |

## Caution

✓ Discriminating against or making any insulting statement about someone else's religion or ethnicity is against the law and could be punishable as a *hate crime*.

# D. Puzzles of American Culture: Basic Values and Unpleasant Realities

These two puzzles show some of the basic American values as well as the unpleasant realities. They will help you begin to understand why Americans think and act the way they do.

## Basic American Values

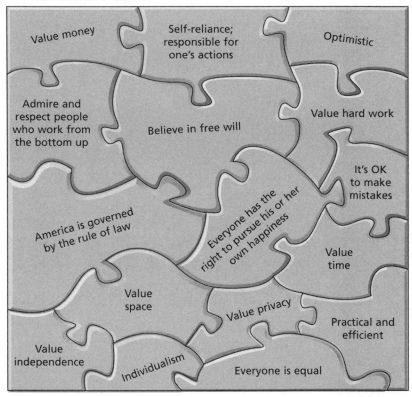

Value money

Self-reliance; responsible for one's actions

Optimistic

Admire and respect people who work from the bottom up

Believe in free will

Value hard work

It's OK to make mistakes

America is governed by the rule of law

Everyone has the right to pursue his or her own happiness

Value time

Value space

Value privacy

Practical and efficient

Value independence

Individualism

Everyone is equal

# Unpleasant Realities

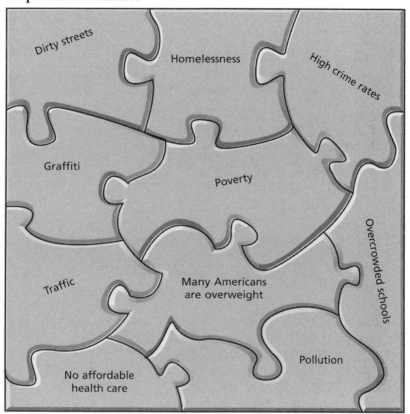

# Body Language

17

# A. Translation of American Body Language

---

*Teacher:*

   *Sometimes you seem very nice, but then you disrespect us by sitting on the desk when you teach. At other times, you look so angry when you put your hands on your waist. That is rude in my country. I am sorry to tell you this, but you make us feel uncomfortable.*

*Thy Khong*

---

Thy Khong,

   I feel terrible that you think I am angry or disrespectful to you. Remember when we talked about communication not just being vocabulary and grammar? I showed the class that interesting fact that 90 percent of face-to-face communication is done with the body and the sound of the voice. Only 10 percent of what we understand is the actual words. We all need to understand the meaning of what our body and voice says to others because it's often very different from culture to culture. When I put my hands on my hips, it means I feel relaxed. This may not be true for everyone. I know it sounds funny, but when you sit in the back of the class with your hands folded across your chest and a very serious look on your face, it makes me feel uncomfortable. When I was a new teacher and students sat like you do, I thought my students were angry with me. Now I know it is just a difference in body languages. Usually, when Americans are angry, they cross their arms tightly against their chest and look very serious. When they are relaxed, they often put their hands on their hips. Of course, it always depends on the situation.

Look at the ads in magazines and on television (especially the fashion ads), and you will see what I mean. The majority of the fashion models will have their hands on their hips, with great big happy smiles.

And why do I sit on the desk? This is not considered rude in America. I sit *on* the desk rather than *behind* the desk because I do not want to put up a wall between us. We are all equal. The only difference between us is that I know more English than you do! So, most of the time, I stand and walk around the classroom; everyone can see me and I can see everyone. But sometimes I get tired and need to sit down. If I sit *behind* the desk, not many students can see me, and I can see only a few in the front. So I sit *on* the desk, and then everyone can see me equally and I can see all of you. In schools in the USA, this is common.

---

 ## P.S.

- ✓ Body language is different in all cultures. Be careful because understanding body language always depends on the whole situation. Be sure to look at the expressions on the face, as well as the body, the sound of the voice, and the words.

But generally:

- ✓ When Americans put their hands on their hips, they are usually relaxed.
- ✓ When Americans fold their arms tightly across their chests, they are angry or very serious (or cold).
- ✓ It is common for an American teacher to sit on the desk.

# B. Personal Space

Dear Teacher,

Can you tell me about how Americans stand in lines? Yesterday I think I made people angry. We were waiting in line for the ATM machine, and the woman in front of me turned around and loudly said something like, "Puh-leeze, sir, give me some room!" I felt so embarrassed, but I wasn't pushing or anything. Then I noticed that the other people in line were standing far away from each other. I know it's a big country, but do people really need so much space? And what is "puh-leeze," it's not in the dictionary.

Sergey

Dear Sergey,

I'm sorry that you had an embarrassing experience, but your observations are very good. I'm glad you are able to tell when people are uncomfortable; that is the first step in translating different body languages.

You're right, Sergey. Lines in the USA are different from lines in other countries. Americans don't stand close in line for the ATM because of the need for safety when they take money out of the machine. They want a lot of space. In the supermarket or at a movie theater, people don't stand as far apart as they do at the ATM, but you should know that Americans value the importance of keeping spaces and never pushing when standing in lines. Also, it is rude to *cut*, or go in front of people in a line. Americans believe in the saying "first come, first served." Everyone must wait his or her turn. Americans like the line to be straight and orderly. Some Americans don't talk to other people in line. In most supermarkets, there are lines for a choice of cashiers. In some stores, banks, and post offices, there is only one line and it leads to several clerks. You might be surprised how patiently Americans will usually wait in line (as long as it's moving).

## Caution

✓ Try not to push or stand too close to people in lines.

✓ It's rude to push into a very crowded elevator. Wait for the next one! When the doors open, you must let the people out before entering. The same is true when waiting for a bus or subway. People first get out, and then the others can get on.

✓ Never *cut*, or go ahead of someone in line.

# C. Touching

*Dear Teacher,*

*I have some new American friends who I like very much, but they make me feel uncomfortable. They are always touching me. When I go to their houses or see them at school, they always give me a hug even if I have just seen them a few days before. Last week, I gave one friend a birthday present. She hugged me when I gave it to her and then she hugged me when she opened it. When I left, everyone at the party gave me another hug. Sometimes while we're talking, they will touch my shoulder. My brother told me to be careful because some women are lesbians (women who love women), and he thinks my friends are this way. But, my friends are always talking about boys. In my country, we never touch people. I like my friends, but I feel so strange with all this touching! What should I do?*

*Sue Hen*

---

Dear Sue Hen,

I think I understand how you feel. I grew up in America, and my friends always touched and hugged each other. When I went to Japan, I saw what it was like in a place where it seemed no one touches (except maybe when the train is too crowded). When I came back to America, I noticed how my friends hugged every time they saw each other or when someone got a gift or gave good news. From what you have told me, I don't think that your friends are lesbians. Nowadays, most gays and lesbians don't feel they need to hide their sexual preference, and they often talk openly about their feelings. You usually don't need to worry about homosexuality being hidden. Your friends sound like perfectly normal, really friendly Americans.

It's true that it might seem that Americans touch each other more than people in your country, but to others, they touch a lot less. It is also true that there may be more hugging in different regions of the United States and among some ethnic groups.

You have several choices about what to do. Try explaining about your culture to your friends and telling them how uncomfortable you feel. You probably won't hurt their feelings, and then you can enjoy being with them without the hugs. However, if you feel too uncomfortable telling them the truth, you can hope that they will read your body language when you pull away from them. Or, you can try to avoid the hugs by walking in the door with something in your hands. Another solution is to do nothing and hope that you will get used to it. Try to enjoy other things about your American friends, and think about how much language and culture you're learning!

 ## P.S.

- ✓ It is common among some Americans to hug a lot. It is okay for women and men to hug each other even if they are just acquaintances (not close friends).
- ✓ Americans often pat (gently hit) people on the back as a sign of encouragement. We even say, "He gave me a pat on the back," meaning that he said good things about me.

## Caution

✓ If a member of the opposite sex (or anyone, for that matter) touches you in a way that makes you uncomfortable, stop that person and say that you are uncomfortable. Tell him or her to stop touching you.

# D. Gestures

*Dear Teacher,*

*This morning my baby and I were disrespected, and by an older woman. Hanon was in her stroller and we were sitting in the park when an older woman walked by. She told me that I had such a cute baby. She started playing a game with Hanon. She said she was going "to get Hanon's nose," and so she pretended to grab my baby's nose with her thumb and two fingers. She did that three times and the third time she said, "Oh look! I have your nose!" She shook her hand at my baby and made a terrible sign. She put her thumb between her two fingers, and she shook her hand like that at Hanon several times, and then she left laughing. I was shaking and went home immediately. Do you think she is a racist?*

*Miki*

---

Dear Miki,

I am sorry that you had such an unpleasant experience. The woman was playing the same game with Hanon that I did with my child and that my mother played with me. We say to the baby, "I'm going to get your nose!" and put the child's nose between our index and middle finger, two times. The third time we do it we show the baby our thumb between the two fingers and say, "And there it is!" The baby thinks the nose is gone and is scared. Then we "put it back," and the baby laughs. Evidently, putting the thumb between the two fingers is rude in your country. Here, it has no meaning except this child's game. The only rude thing the woman did was to touch your child without asking permission. It is not okay for a stranger to touch a baby or child.

*Dear Teacher,*

*You tell us to always keep our eyes open and to question, question, question. So let me tell you that yesterday I was shocked when you told us how tall your little daughter was and the size of your dog. You held your hand in the same position for both of them! We never do that in my country. It is so disrespectful. We show a person's height with the fingers of the hand pointing straight to the ceiling. For an animal, the hand is flat, palm down like you did for your daughter. To show the table height, we put our hand sideways. You also count with your hands differently than we do. Did I observe correctly and is that normal American culture?*

*Roberto*

---

Dear Roberto,

Congratulations on your observations. If you had asked your excellent questions during the class, then I could have shared the explanation with everyone. Yes, we use the same hand signal to show height for people, animals, and things. We simply put our hand at the specific height with the palm of the hand facing the floor. I didn't know that you would do it differently. Maybe it's just our idea of equality! And, yes, I have noticed that people in each culture use their hands differently to count. I always start with the thumb of my left hand, palm facing me, and raise each finger in order. Then I count the rest of the numbers on my right hand, if I need to get to ten. Remind me to have the class all count together tomorrow. It'll be fun to see all the different ways!

*Dear Teacher,*

*The way Americans use their hands is strange. Yesterday, my roommate told me to go away, but she meant come here. People put their hands in their pockets while they stand and talk to me, which is rude in my country. Also, when I pointed at someone with my middle finger, he got really upset.*

*Erika*

---

Dear Erika,

Gestures (the way we use our hands to communicate) are very different from country to country. In the U.S., the sign for "come here" is to put your palm up, facing you, at face level, and move your fingers toward your face. If someone points at you with only the index finger, it is often rude. However, it is common for Americans to shake their index fingers in the air when making a strong point. It means, "Listen to me. This is very important." Showing only your middle finger is a very rude gesture, and you should never point that finger directly at someone.

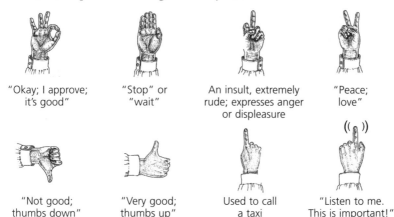

| "Okay; I approve; it's good" | "Stop" or "wait" | An insult, extremely rude; expresses anger or displeasure | "Peace; love" |

| "Not good; thumbs down" | "Very good; thumbs up" | Used to call a taxi | "Listen to me. This is important!" |

## P.S.

- ✓ It's not rude to blow your nose in public, but don't do it too loudly. You must use a handkerchief or tissue (not your fingers).

- ✓ To point to an object, use your index finger. To make an important point, move your index finger up and down or sideways. But be careful, and don't point directly at a person.

- ✓ When someone looks or points in our direction and we are not sure if they really want us, we usually point with our index finger to our chest. We tilt our head (move our head to the side) a little, use a questioning look, and say, "Me?"

- ✓ Waving your hand from side to side, palm facing out, means "no" or "go away."

- ✓ Holding your hand up with the palm facing forward but no movement means "stop."

# Caution

- ✓ Americans might wink at you (close one eye and keep the other eye open). This is usually a signal of a joke or a shared amusement. However, if there is no joke and a man winks at a woman (or vice versa), it is considered not appropriate because it might be sexual. Remember that understanding body language always depends on the situation.

- ✓ Never put your fingers in your nose (pick your nose) in public.

- ✓ Some Americans feel that it is rude to use a toothpick in public, even if you hide your hand with a napkin.

- ✓ It's rude to spit in public. (But you will see athletes on TV do this.)

- ✓ Some people consider it rude to put your fingers in your mouth (as in chewing fingernails).

- ✓ Never show your fist with the middle finger extended. This is an insult.

- ✓ Shaking a closed fist at someone is also rude, especially if it is in someone's face. This is an expression of anger.

- ✓ It is rude to stare (look for a long time) or whistle (make music with your lips) at any man or woman you don't know.

# Social Customs and Manners

# A. Smiling Faces

*Teacher:*

*I don't want to be rude, but Americans are so phony. They seem false. They smile all the time. They say "Hi" to strangers. Yesterday an older woman on the bus told me her first name and then talked all about her divorce and her problems with her ex-husband. I had never seen her before! At college, I met a nice classmate, and we talked and talked. We exchanged phone numbers, and she said, "Let's meet for lunch." It's been three weeks, and she has never called.*

*Natasha*

---

Dear Natasha,

You are not the first student to be surprised by how often Americans smile and talk to strangers. You are asking if friendly Americans are really honest. The answer is that Americans are not phony or insincere when they meet strangers. Most Americans are friendly and do smile a lot. By the way, it's hard to speak clear English without putting your mouth in a smile! Americans are typically happy to meet other people; and you see that in smiles and friendly talk.

In America, it is important to be friendly and curious and to start conversations with strangers. As you have experienced, Americans sometimes ask people (even new people they have just met on the bus, standing in line at the bank, or at a party) personal questions. Of course, Natasha, if it makes you uncomfortable, you don't have to answer the questions. You can quickly change the subject by asking them another question, or just be honest and say, "I feel uncomfortable talking about that." Most Americans are not afraid of sharing a little bit of their lives with others. Just be careful to never ask Americans about their age, religion, money, or weight. These topics are *taboo* (not talked about) in America. This tradition comes from the first colonists (the people who came to America from England in the 1600s) who wanted freedom to choose a new life that did not depend on their religion, their age, or their class in society.

Often an American you meet will say, "We must get together for lunch soon," but that person never calls you. This is not insincere. At the time the person said it, he or she really meant it. As the days go by, though, there is never enough time to do the things everyone needs or wants to do. So time passes and no call is made. Many Americans work a lot and schedule too many things in too little time. Many Americans do not have the time to just relax and meet friends as much as they would like to.

## P.S.

- ✓ Americans tend to smile a lot.
- ✓ Americans are friendly and sometimes talk to strangers.
- ✓ Americans sometimes share personal stories with strangers.

# B. "How Are You?"

*Dear Teacher,*

*It took me such a long time to figure out that when Americans say, "How are you?" they don't really care about the answer. It seems so dishonest. People also say, "What's up?" "How you doing?" "What's happening?" and "How's it going?" and it seems like they just mean, "Hi." When I first got here, I thought people actually cared how I was feeling and what was happening in my life. I was embarrassed a few times because I started telling them what was going on with me and they were already walking away! Are Americans really so insincere? If I honestly want to know how someone is doing, what do I say?*

*Ralf*

Dear Ralf,

It is strange that Americans' standard greeting does not really translate word for word. I guess it's just tradition. "How are you?" really just means "I see you and I greet you." It's like a dog wagging (moving) his tail at another dog and then walking away. It's usually a little rude to not say "How are you?" even when you see the same people every day. People often have this type of conversation while walking past each other. It is simply a form of greeting and not a question about health at all. Asking how someone is feeling isn't really the purpose. The important thing is not the question. What is important is that when you see people, you immediately greet them with a smile and some words. Often, people will start a conversation with "How are you?" and, if there is time, begin to talk seriously. If you really want to know how someone is feeling, you can ask a second question after the first:

"Hi, how are you?"
"Good, how about you?"
"I'm all right. So what have you been up to?" Or "Is everything going well with you?"

When a second question is asked after the first greeting, it becomes clear that it isn't just an ordinary greeting but a real question and the beginning of a conversation.

---

## P.S.

✓ Asking "How are you?" is simply a greeting and not a question about your health.

# C. Eating in Restaurants

*Teacher,*

*I went to my first American restaurant and it was so confusing! Just as I sat down a man put ice water and bread and butter on the table. I hadn't ordered that, so I immediately sent it back. When he explained that there was no charge for water or bread, I felt so embarrassed! Then the waitress came and was smiling and she was very friendly. She said "Hi, my name is Susie and I will be your server tonight." Teacher, in my country the waiters never act like that. And then when she asked if I wanted soup or salad she made me crazy. The choices! There were four kinds of soup, and when I decided on a salad, she wanted to know what dressing and there were six different kinds. She asked me how I wanted my steak cooked: "well, medium, or rare." I didn't understand that at all. She asked if I wanted a baked potato, boiled potatoes, fried potatoes, mashed potatoes, or rice. I was exhausted by all the choices and so nervous. It was like taking a test! Teacher, is this normal?*

*Joey*

---

Dear Joey,

It was wonderful for me to read your letter because I have never thought of these things before. Yes, your experience was normal, and I hope the next time you can be prepared for the differences in culture and enjoy yourself and your meal. Servers earn most of their money from their tips, so they try to be very friendly and helpful. Because America is the land of choices, Susie gave you choices on types of soup or dressings. It is also common for the customer to ask the server for details of the ingredients and his or her opinion about the food. Americans commonly ask the server, "What would you recommend?" or "Is there anything special tonight?" or "What is in that?"

If there is something wrong with the food, you should send it back. You will not be expected to pay for it. It's considered polite to leave a tip of 15–20 percent of the total bill. (It is not normal for the restaurant to include the tip in the bill unless it is a large group of people.) If the service is bad, some people don't leave a good tip. Be sure to tell the manager about the poor service. When it comes to ordering meat at a restaurant, the server will ask, "How do you like the meat cooked?" *Well* means that the meat is cooked a long time and looks almost brown inside, *medium* means there is a little pink color on the inside, and *rare* means that it is not cooked very much—brown on the outside but red on the inside.

---

*Teacher,*

*I met an American at my church, and she invited me to meet her at a restaurant for lunch. She seemed like a very nice, polite woman, but her manners were very bad! When her food came, she just sat there talking to me and did not start eating. She didn't eat until my food came. Then, she had her fork in her right hand and her left hand was under the table! My mother always taught me that both hands must be above the table when we eat. I know I was rude, but I kept staring at how she ate. First, the fork was in her right hand, then, when she cut her food, she put the fork in her left hand and her knife in her right. When she was finished cutting, she put the knife on her plate and her fork in her right hand, her left hand back under the table, and then she ate. It made me dizzy (to feel like the room is moving around). And, she kept talking while we were eating. She would ask me a question, and then put food in her mouth. That is very rude in my country. First we eat, and then, when we are finished, we can talk. She asked the waiter to put the food she didn't finish in a "doggie bag" (little box to take home). I felt so ashamed. We would never do that in my country. It shows that you are poor. Is she polite or rude?*

*Shoshana*

---

Dear Shoshana,

Thank you for your detailed observations. Yes, your new American friend sounds very polite by American standards. My mother always taught me to eat with one hand under the table when I wasn't cutting my food. I think that Americans are the only people who eat that way! It may seem odd how Americans keep changing hands using forks and knives, but if that's what our mothers taught us, then that's the right thing to do! It is considered rude to start eating before anyone else at the table. This is why she waited for your food to be served to you. She was probably waiting for you to tell her, "Please start eating before me or it will get cold," and then she could eat. It is common to take food home. If it tastes good, we don't want to waste it, and we will eat it later as "leftovers." We call it a doggie bag because we used to pretend we were taking it for our dog. Now we are proud to say that because the food is so delicious we want to finish it later.

Americans often meet people for breakfast, lunch, or dinner because we work a lot, and meal times are often the only chance we have to talk. So we ask a question, put the food in our mouth, chew, and listen. It's kind of like a dance. One eats while the other talks, and vice versa. It is polite (and expected) to talk while eating, but *never* when there is food in your mouth.

*Dear Teacher,*

*I can't believe how rude my American friend is. He said that he wanted to have dinner with me. Then, when the bill came, he looked surprised when I didn't put down any money. He told me how much my share was! In my country, the man always pays for the woman. Also, he's older than I am. If I had known I was going to have to pay, I would not have ordered the steak or had a second glass of wine. I can't believe how impolite he is and I told him I don't want to see him again.*

*Ofelia*

---

Ofelia,

I am glad you told me about this. Americans normally think that everyone will pay for him or herself, even if it is a date (and I am not clear if it was or not). In the USA, remember that Americans value equality. The words "Let's meet for dinner," "Let's have dinner together," or "Please join me" don't necessarily mean that the other person will pay. The words that usually mean the person wants to pay are, "It's my treat" or "I'm taking you to dinner." If someone "treats" you, that means that he or she plans to pay for everything. In America, treating the other person is usually done for special occasions like a birthday or to thank the person for something he or she did. Who pays does not depend on gender or age. In America, we are all equal.

There is a general idea in America that the bill will be shared or split. This is called *going Dutch.* Americans don't often mention this before the meal because it is generally understood.

If someone does offer to *treat* you, it's polite to be careful about what you order. You might want to ask what the other person is ordering and then order something that is the same price or less expensive. It is considered very impolite and rude to order the most expensive thing on the menu because the other person is paying. If someone offers to pay at the end, it is polite to try to argue at first: "No, no, let me get it," or to question the person: "Are you sure?" A compromise is to ask if you can pay for the tip or buy dessert, coffee, or a drink at the next location. It's also okay to simply say, "Thank you," as long as you don't act like you were expecting it.

---

 **P.S.**

- ✓ Ice water is typically served when you sit down in restaurants. However, this may begin to change due to concerns about wasting water.

- ✓ Bread is often put on the table, and there is usually no charge.

- ✓ The server should be very friendly and helpful and often will tell you his or her name.

- ✓ When the service is good, tipping is expected to be 15–20 percent of the bill.

- ✓ You will be offered many different choices in your order— choices of soup, salad dressing, potatoes, vegetables, how your meat will be cooked, etc.

- ✓ Salad is eaten before the main course.

- ✓ Coffee is often served with and after your meal.

- ✓ It is normal for servers to ask you if you want to take your uneaten food home in a *doggie bag*. If they don't ask, you can ask them.

- ✓ If the food is not good, send it back. Don't eat too much of it.
- ✓ If there are any problems with the food or service, politely tell the manager.
- ✓ In most states, smoking is not allowed inside any restaurant or bar. Be sure to ask before lighting your cigarette.
- ✓ Polite Americans eat with one hand, while the other one is under the table on their laps.
- ✓ Usually, when friends meet at restaurants, they each pay their share of the bill or split the bill in half: It's called *going Dutch*.
- ✓ When you want the server to bring the check, make a writing gesture with one hand as if you are holding a pen and hold out the other hand as if it were paper. If you just want the server to come, try to make eye contact and raise your hand when he or she looks your way.
- ✓ If you are confused about how or what to order when you are in a restaurant or about tipping, ask the server.

## Caution

- ✓ If you are in a very nice restaurant and the server asks if you want water, be sure you say "tap" water (city water from the kitchen faucet). If you don't, you might get bottled water, which could cost about $5–7. The city water throughout the USA is healthy to drink.

# P.P.S. Tipping for Other Services

- ✓ Leave 15–20 percent of the bill if you receive good service in a nice restaurant.

- ✓ A tip for a taxi driver is usually 15 percent of the bill. You can give 20 percent if the driver gets you there quickly or 10 percent if the ride is bad. If the driver is rude or a bad driver, leave no tip. Be sure to copy the driver's name to contact the taxi company (but be sure to get your suitcases out of the trunk of the taxi first).

- ✓ If you are staying in a nice hotel and someone carries your luggage to your room, the tip is usually $1–2 a bag. This is also true for baggage handlers at the airport or train station.

- ✓ If you need to check your coat at a restaurant, and there is no charge to do that, a tip of $1 per coat is nice.

- ✓ For barbers, hair stylists, masseuses (someone who rubs your body for relaxation or to remove pain), or manicurists (someone who decorates nails), a tip of 15 percent of the bill is expected.

- ✓ For valet parking, the tip is usually $1 over the parking charge.

- ✓ At the holidays Americans generally leave a card with $5–20 for their letter carriers, newspaper delivery persons, gardeners, pet sitters, house cleaners, or anyone who provides a service throughout the year.

# D. Being Invited or Inviting Americans to the Home

*Dear Teacher,*

*I'm so confused. My American classmate told me several times that we should get together "sometime." She said that if I was ever in "the neighborhood" (she lives near campus) that I should stop by. Yesterday I was at school and I had two hours before my next class, so I decided to visit her. I thought we could have lunch, so I picked up some sandwiches.*

*When I got to her house, she didn't seem very happy to see me. She was wearing her pajamas, and it was 12:00 in the afternoon. At first it seemed like she wasn't even going to invite me in. Then she did. I told her that we could have lunch, and she seemed confused. She asked if we had made plans, and I told her that I thought she had told me to stop by. She told me that she was really sorry, but she couldn't have lunch because she had to take a shower and get ready for school. I thought she was really rude and I think she was really angry with me. Why did she say something she didn't mean?*

*Selma*

---

Dear Selma,

You didn't understand what she actually meant. Americans may seem insincere because often they will say things like, "Let's get together sometime" or "If you're ever in my neighborhood, you should stop by," but then never make plans. It can be very confusing. When people say these things, they mean them, at that moment. Americans feel a need to be friendly and social but, realistically, often have little time to be social. When your classmate said you should come by, she probably meant that you should make plans for you to come by some time. Or, if you're ever in the neighborhood, that you should call first and find out if it's convenient to come over. If it isn't, then plans can be made for another time. Most Americans don't like surprises, and if they are going to have guests, they want to know ahead of time so they can prepare. She was probably embarrassed because you saw her in pajamas at noon, and she was surprised to see you at her door. If you want to continue the friendship, just tell her that you are so sorry that you misunderstood and that you'd like to have lunch with her sometime. Suggest several possible dates to get together, and let her choose what works best for her.

---

 ## P.S.

*Here are some tips if you have guests over to your house:*

✓ Turn off your television. Make sure your music isn't too loud. The reason Americans invite people to come to their houses is to talk and get to know each other better.

✓ Make the guests comfortable and offer them something to drink. Often, Americans will give the guest a tour of the house.

*Here are some tips if you are a guest in someone's house:*

✓ Never just "drop in" (go to the home without calling). Call from your cell phone if you are in the neighborhood.

✓ Come on time. Americans are uncomfortable when people come early or too late. See more on this on pages 45–49.

# E. American Parties

*Teacher,*

*Last Saturday night I went to an American party. It was so strange. A few weeks ago, I got an invitation in the mail from my friend at work. It wasn't for a birthday or anniversary; it just said, "Please come to a dinner party at 6:30."*

*When I got there, and he opened the door, he seemed a little surprised and angry. He looked at his watch, and then he looked at me and my sister, her husband, and my little nephew. When we went in, everyone was eating dessert and sitting around talking. It was really boring. There wasn't any music or dancing, just talking, and there wasn't any dinner, either. Everyone left early, about 10:00, and we left because we were hungry.*

*He is no longer friendly at work and I think I did something wrong but I don't know what. Can you help?*

*Victor*

---

Victor,

Yes, I think you did a lot of things wrong. First, did the invitation have the letters RSVP followed by his phone number? Those letters mean that you must telephone (or tell him at work) if you will come or not. It is very rude not to RSVP to an invitation. If you didn't tell him, then he probably thought you weren't coming.

Next, as with many things in the USA like employment interviews or appointments, it is very important to come to a party on time. This is especially important if it is a dinner party or a surprise party. The invitation said 6:30, and you were expected to be there at 6:30.

You are not supposed to arrive earlier or later! (If the invitation says "Open house: 2 PM to 6 PM" or "Cocktail party: 8 PM to midnight," that means you can come anytime **between** those times). You didn't tell me what time you arrived, but it must have been around 8:30 PM because everyone was already finished with dinner and was eating dessert. If your co-worker thought you were coming, he would have waited for you for about a half hour before he served the food. When a guest comes late, often the host will wait to serve and the food will get cold or be overcooked. If your friend didn't think you were coming, he might have been embarrassed or angry when he saw you at 8:30 because he might not have had enough food and certainly he would not have had a special place for you to sit.

You said that you were there with your sister and brother-in-law and little nephew. Were they invited too? It is considered really rude to go to any kind of party with uninvited friends or family, without first asking the permission of the host or hostess, in advance. An invitation is for the person whose name is on it, and for that person only, unless followed by *Guest*. Then it means you can bring one person. How old is your nephew? Americans do not bring children to any party unless it is a children's birthday or a family event.

He served you dessert and not dinner because the dinner was already finished. I'm glad you left with the other guests. American parties do not last all night, and it is rude for a guest to stay later than the end time of the party.

I'm sorry that you were bored, but the main purpose of most American parties is to meet new people, so you must be able to talk. You need to make *small talk*—talk about things in the news, the weather, or sports. This helps you find out if you have anything in common. Because of this need to have a real conversation, there is rarely loud music or dancing at a typical American party. You were lucky that you could sit down. At a cocktail party or open house, there are fewer chairs than people on purpose. If you sit down, you cannot walk around to meet new people.

You didn't tell me if you brought him anything. When you're invited to an American party, you don't *have* to bring anything, but it's nice to bring some flowers, a bottle of wine, or some candy for the host or hostess. Because this is simply a way of saying "thank you for inviting me," don't spend more than $10 on the gift or you might make the host or hostess uncomfortable.

So, Victor, if these descriptions fit what happened, go to your co-worker and apologize. Tell him the truth. Tell him that in your culture, you are expected to come late and bring friends, family, and children. Tell him that you didn't know that American culture was so different, but now you know. Ask him if you can take him to lunch.

 ## P.S.

- ✓ Americans have parties for many different reasons.
- ✓ The majority of American parties are not to celebrate a birthday or anniversary. In fact, some parties are held for no special reason at all, except for friends to get together and meet new people.
- ✓ For most parties, you are invited by the host or hostess by a telephone call, email, or written invitation.
- ✓ If you receive a written invitation, you are asked to RSVP. This means you must telephone (or write) and say if you can come or not. You should not change your mind.

- ✓ A cocktail party or an open house will be held from one specific time to another. The invitation will say "between 2 PM and 6 PM" or "between 8 PM and midnight," so you can come anytime between those times.

- ✓ At a cocktail party or an open house, there will not be a dinner. There will be some *finger food* to eat (no plates or forks, just use your fingers and a napkin): cheese and crackers, potato chips and dip, or raw vegetables and dip. There will probably be wine and beer (some sort of alcohol) and bottled water to drink.

- ✓ Another kind of party is a *potluck*. You will be expected to bring a food to share or a *dish to pass*. The host or hostess will often tell you what to bring.

- ✓ Because of this need to have a real conversation, there is rarely loud music or dancing at a typical American party. There are always very few chairs. If you sit down, you cannot walk around to meet new people, and you might have to sit next to someone who isn't interesting.

- ✓ When you go to an American party, it's nice to bring some flowers, a bottle of wine, or some candy for the host or hostess. Because this is simply a way of saying thank you for inviting me, spending more than $10 on the gift might make the host or hostess feel uncomfortable.

## Caution

- ✓ At most American parties, children are definitely not included, nor are family members. You must never bring any uninvited friends, children, or family with you without first asking the permission of the host or hostess. Americans hire babysitters to take care of their children at their home so they can go out to parties, movies, etc.

- ✓ It is very rude not to RSVP to an invitation.

- ✓ If the invitation to the party says 7 PM, you are expected to be there at 7 PM. Do not arrive earlier, and do not come later!

- ✓ Never stay later than the end time of the party. When other people start to leave, you should leave too. It's not good to be the last one at a party.

# F. What to Wear

Dear Teacher,

I am so confused about what I wear. Last Sunday, my American friend invited me to a barbeque. It was a nice summer day, so I put on a pretty summer dress and high heels. When I got to the barbeque, I realized I was overdressed. Some women told me my dress was nice, but I was embarrassed. The other women were wearing jeans, shorts, and t-shirts. My heels sank into the grass and got dirty. It was difficult to walk around. The next weekend, my American friend invited me to a party on Saturday night. I remembered my big mistake the week before, so I wore jeans and a t-shirt. Oh, Teacher, imagine how I felt when we got to the party and all the girls were wearing nice dresses and high heels! I felt so out of place. I saw some of the same people from the barbeque. They must have thought I was crazy!

Yesterday, because it's summer, I wore a new dress to work. I don't know what was wrong, but I felt that what I was wearing wasn't right for work because men were looking at me funny and women were not looking at me at all. I guess my skirt was a little short and the top was a little low, but I wore those same style clothes to work all the time in my country. I've noticed that the American women don't wear high heels at work, and several have asked me how I can walk in them all day. I'm surprised that they wear such ugly shoes, but I want them to like me. Teacher, how do I know what to wear?

Maria

50

Dear Maria,

This same kind of thing also happens to Americans. Most of the time, you should wear what you feel comfortable in, but be sure to ask your American friend what other people will be wearing to the event. Generally speaking, events in the day are more casual than events at night. Also consider what kind of party it is and where it is. If it's an outside party, people usually dress more comfortably. If it's inside and at night, people might dress up a little more. As you've noticed, Americans are usually more casual than people from other countries. However, Americans often admire others when they are nicely dressed. When you went to the barbeque, the women who said you looked nice probably wished that they had worn nicer dresses. Your only mistake was wearing high heels on grass. So if you want to wear something nice, you should if you feel comfortable.

What you wear to work is different. Your job might have a specific dress code. Check with a co-worker. If there isn't a dress code, don't wear what you would wear to a party. You don't want to dress in a way that is distracting and that could cause problems in the workplace. Most of all at work, look at what your co-workers wear, and try to dress like them. This doesn't mean you have to wear "ugly" shoes, but find some shoes you think are nice that don't have such high heels.

---

*Dear Teacher,*

*I want to thank you so much for what you did yesterday. When you took me outside to explain what my t-shirt said, I thought I would die. You were so sweet to suggest that I just go to the restroom and turn it inside out. I still feel so embarrassed! I want to just throw it away, but I can't. Can you believe, Teacher, my mother gave it to me as a present when she*

*came back from San Francisco! I'll never be able to tell her what the English meant. Thank you so much for your kindness to me.*

*Ani*

---

Dear Ani,

It was not easy for me to tell you the meaning of your shirt. But, if I didn't, then you would have continued wearing it and maybe some stranger would have told you. Be sure that you check with me or a native speaker whenever you wear anything that has English words on it. And warn all your friends, too!

---

*Dear Teacher,*

*I need to tell you the truth. I left class yesterday because you asked me to take off my cap and my hair was so messy. I felt embarrassed and angry. Lots of people wear caps. Why don't you allow it in class?*

*Eddy*

---

Dear Eddy,

Thank you for your note. I knew you were upset when you left, and I am happy that you told me how you feel. You know I don't allow anyone to wear baseball caps in class; I tell the women as well. I know that in the past 20 years, American fashion has made it common for men and women to wear baseball caps. First, the style was the bill faced front, and then it faced back. Now it seems that it is worn sideways or in the front again. However, in average American culture, it is still considered rude to wear hats in any inside space (except for a religious purpose): an office, school, restaurant, etc. I want to teach my students what is considered appropriate and polite in average society. It's a free country, of course, so outside of my class, you can make decisions about what you want to do. Recently, it seems to be more and more common for banks, large office buildings, airports, and places where security is important to ask people to remove their hats and sunglasses before entering those places. Also, when they take your photograph for your bus pass, driver's license, passport, etc., they will ask you to take off your hat.

---

 ## P.S.

- ✓ If you are worried about what to wear to a party, the best thing to do is ask what you should wear when you RSVP (call the host to say that you are coming). They might say *casual* (relaxed, informal) or *dressy* or *black tie* (like at a wedding). If you are unsure, describe what you plan to wear, and ask if that is okay.

- ✓ For a swimming party or a beach party, you would wear a bathing suit. But be sure to bring something to cover yourself in case it gets too sunny or too windy or if there will be food. A shirt works for a man. A robe, blouse, or a *sarong* (a long piece of fabric you can wrap around yourself) works for a woman.

- ✓ For a picnic, shorts or jeans are fine, depending on the weather.

✓ For a casual party at someone's home, wear clothes you are comfortable in. Women can add some jewelry and a little more make-up.

✓ At a more formal party or event, men should wear a suit and tie and white or blue shirt; women should wear a nice dress or a very nice pant suit.

✓ Black tie parties are not too common. They are usually formal weddings. *Black tie* means that the men should wear a tuxedo (usually rented) or suit and the women should wear a long, very fancy dress.

# G. Things We Don't Talk About

*Dear Teacher,*

*My brother is married to an American woman, so I was invited to a small party at their new house. I tried being friendly to the people there, but they were not friendly to me. I know I did some things wrong, but I don't know what. One woman was really pretty so I asked her how old she was. She just stared at me and said, "Old enough" and walked away. I went to the wine table and said hello to a man. He asked me what I did. I told him I didn't know what I did to make her walk away. He looked at me very strangely. I noticed that he was wearing a really nice Rolex watch. To be polite, I asked him how much it cost. He said, "Just enough" and then he, too, walked away. I was feeling kind of bad, so I went over to an older couple and I tried to talk to them. I told them all about my country and the church I go to. Then I asked them what church they went to. They seemed angry and didn't answer my question. They asked me if I liked the taste of the appetizers (finger foods). It was strange, and I felt really uncomfortable. What did I do wrong?*

*Abner*

---

Dear Abner,

Uh oh! You made several social mistakes! In America, it is rude to directly ask about someone's age or religion or to ask them anything about money—like how much something he or she owns costs. Sometimes even close friends don't talk about those topics in public.

With the older couple, besides invading their privacy by asking about their religion, you probably talked too much about yourself. When polite Americans meet strangers, we take turns talking. It's

55

very much like playing tennis or ping pong. You should have asked him or her a question (you throw the ball) and then listened to the answer. If the couple wanted to continue talking to you, they would have asked you a question (they throw the ball back) and listened to your answer. Then you should have tried to keep the conversation going (throwing the ball) back and forth. When one of the people keeps talking (keeps the ball), that means he or she really doesn't want to "play" the conversation game.

Abner, you could have started the conversation with a safe topic like asking about the weather or sports. We call that *small talk*. After the small talk, an American usually asks, "What do you do?" That is what the man with the Rolex watch probably asked you. His question was really asking about the kind of job you have. He didn't mean, "What did you do to make the woman so angry?" Because most Americans can choose the kind of work that interests them, telling him what you do would have let him know a little about your personality and if you both had something in common.

I'm sorry you had such an embarrassing time, but next time it will be better. By the way, what kind of appetizers did they have?

---

*Dear Teacher,*

*Today when you said that Americans are really uncomfortable talking about age, religion, money, or weight, I realized what I did wrong last week at work. I have an American co-worker that I like a lot (just as a friend). We talk and laugh together all the time. Last week I saw her and said, "Hey Gordita." She knows a little Spanish and understood that I called her "fatty." She got very angry and told me I was annoying and rude. She has not talked to me since. Teacher, in my country, we often call our friends that word, but now I know that calling her that made her feel*

*bad. (She is a little overweight.) What can I do? I want to apologize, but I don't want to make it worse. Would flowers help?*

*Elmer*

---

Dear Elmer:

You certainly did hurt her feelings by calling her "fatty"—it just doesn't translate well in English. Americans are very sensitive about their weight and feel that is a very private matter. I suggest you just tell her the truth. Tell her you are really sorry that you said what you did and that in Spanish that term is one of friendship. If talking directly to her makes you uncomfortable, you can write her a note. Flowers are a nice idea but make them small and inexpensive. Maybe a cute little potted plant. Don't spend more than $7–8. Good luck.

---

## P.S.

- ✓ When you meet Americans, be sure to look them in the eye and smile.
- ✓ Most Americans shake hands on meeting.
- ✓ Make small talk at the beginning of a conversation.
- ✓ After a few questions, expect to be asked, "What do you do?" Maybe you will find that you have something in the common with the person.

# Caution

- ✓ Never ask Americans about their religion.
- ✓ Never ask Americans how old they are.
- ✓ Never ask Americans about their weight or dress/suit or shoe size.
- ✓ Do not ask Americans anything about money: how much they make or how much their car, house, or clothes cost. If you feel you need to know, ask, "Was it expensive?" That gives them the choice to say just yes or no or to give you the details.
- ✓ Do not say anything negative about someone's religion or their heritage (family background) or about any race.
- ✓ Do not say anything sexist—anything that would suggest that women aren't equal to men. Do not make any anti-homosexual comments either.
- ✓ Americans say that they don't want to talk about politics, but sometimes they do. It's best to just listen first to see the other person's point of view and how strongly he or she feels before you let them know your thoughts. Some Americans are more open to disagreement on politics than other people.

# Relationships

# A. Dating

*Dear Teacher,*

*I'm dating an American woman, and I don't understand her. We've had three dates. The first two times, she let me pay, but last time, she insisted on paying for my dinner! In my country, this is the man's job. When she pays the bill, it makes me feel uncomfortable. Also, she has several male "friends," whom she talks about when we are together. That is so rude and impolite! I should be the only man in her life. I don't know if we should continue seeing each other or if she is interested in me at all.*

*Raul*

Dear Raul,

Dating can be very confusing. It is important to know that in the U.S. people want to be treated equally. This is true especially now that the majority of American women have jobs and their own money. A lot of American women do not feel comfortable having the man pay all the time. It is nice that you bought her dinner twice, but now she wants to show you that she is not using you. She wants to make the relationship equal. It is not unusual for a woman to *treat* (pay for) her date, especially after he has already paid a few times. If the woman doesn't pay for dinner, she often pays for something else, like dessert, coffee, or drinks to show that she doesn't expect the man to pay for everything. This is considered polite because having one person pay for everything creates an imbalance, which makes Americans feel unequal and uncomfortable.

It is often surprising to many foreigners that men and women in America have good, close, non-sexual friendships with each other and are sometimes roommates. Having a friend or co-worker of the opposite sex does not necessarily mean that there is any sexual interest. The woman you are dating does not mean to make you feel bad by talking about her male friends. She probably wants to share a part of her life with you. I cannot tell you if you should continue to see each other. However, it is important for you to not be too jealous or possessive of American women. The majority of American women want to have independent lives outside of their boyfriends' (and/or husbands') lives, and if you think you should be the *only* man in her life, you might have problems. However, if you really like her and are willing to accept her and open yourself to her American culture, it might work out.

---

*Dear Teacher,*

*I enrolled in an online dating service on the Internet. At first, I just wanted to know more about what people do online. I thought I could learn something new about American culture. I chose a plan for three months. I have been opening and reading a lot of profiles where people show a picture and give information about themselves. Some men wrote very nice ones, but some are too sexy with their pictures and words. Some people have been contacting me by email, and I am doing the same, too. It was fun at first, but I feel that maybe they are not honest. I have never dated anyone before. Do you think I can trust what they say?*

*Fatima*

---

Oh, Fatima, be careful! You are absolutely right that some people seem to be nice with their online descriptions, while others can make you feel afraid. Please be careful because you still don't know what is considered normal in American culture. If you find someone you think is interesting, you could plan to meet him, but only at a public place, like Starbucks. The same would be true if you met someone who seemed nice on the bus or at a party. Be sure never to get into a car of a stranger or invite someone you don't know to your home.

You can give a stranger your first name, maybe even your phone number and email, but never your home address. Unlike other countries, in America, "nice" girls sometimes talk and smile at strangers. After meeting someone a few times in a public place, you should be able to tell if you can trust him. But do it slowly, and as I said before, be careful. Good luck!

 **P.S.**

- ✓ It is normal for American women to have male friends who are just friends (and vice versa).
- ✓ It is not uncommon for American men and women to share an apartment and not have a sexual relationship with each other.
- ✓ Most American women do not like possessive or jealous men.
- ✓ Most American women do not feel comfortable having the man pay for everything all of the time.
- ✓ There are hundreds of dating services in the USA. Combined they generate millions of dollars.
- ✓ When dating, get to know the person slowly. Be careful not to talk only about yourself on the first date.

## Caution

- ✓ A lot of people don't tell the truth on their online profile in dating services. They often lie about their age, job, and whether or not they are single. It can't hurt to "talk" to someone online, and it is a wonderful way to meet people. Just be careful!

- ✓ Meet your new friend in a public place many times before you get into a car or give out your address. (This is true whether it is a man or a woman—a stranger is a stranger.)

# B. Marriage and In-Laws

*Dear Teacher,*

*I'm embarrassed to tell you that my American co-worker found me crying yesterday. I explained that my mother-in-law, who lives with us, has never been nice to me and it is getting worse. She is always telling me what to do and then she says that everything I do is wrong. My co-worker looked surprised and said that she would never permit her mother-in-law to tell her what to do and would never allow her mother-in-law to live with her. She asked me what my husband says, but I explained that she is his mother, so he supports her. My co-worker said that in America a husband's first loyalty is to his wife and his second loyalty is to his children, not his mother. She said that her mother-in-law was very sweet. She laughed and said that American mothers-in-law know that if they are not nice to their daughters-in-law (or, she added, to their sons-in-law), they know they will not be invited to visit their sons (or daughters) or see their grandchildren. So they are usually very nice and friendly. I can't believe this. Is this normal?*

*June*

---

Dear June,

I'm sorry that you are having such a bad time with your mother-in-law. Yes, your co-worker is right. In the majority of families in the USA, the husband and wife respect and care for each other first; their loyalty is to each other. If a member of one of the families, especially the mother-in-law, is not nice to the other spouse (the husband or wife), or if that person criticizes or makes trouble, then the son or daughter stops it or the parent will not be included in most family

64

gatherings (usually with the exception of holidays). Have you ever seen the television situation comedy "Everybody Loves Raymond"? One of the reasons it was such a popular program was because of the relationships between Raymond and his wife (Deborah) and his mother, who lived across the street. A major part of the comedy was that, in America, it is not normal for in-laws to live so close (and rarely do in-laws live in the home of the son and daughter-in-law). June, my own mother-in-law was always sweet to me. I think she was typical. She treated me with respect because she knew that if she wasn't nice to me, she wouldn't be seeing her son or grandchildren very often. Try talking to your husband, and ask if he can give you more support in this case. He needs to know how unhappy you are.

---

*Dear Teacher,*

*You told us to read advice columns to learn about American culture. Well, if "Ask Amy" is true, American culture is really terrible. People live together before they get married and half of the people get divorced. The man gets no respect because he is supposed to help with the woman's jobs in the kitchen as well as help take care of the children. Yesterday, the letter was all about the husband taking off a year of work to take care of the children while his wife worked as a lawyer. Is all of this true? How do the American men allow this to happen?*

*George*

Dear George,

Well, what you read in the advice columns is typical American values and true. Americans don't think that it's bad for a husband to help in the kitchen or to take care of the children; it is often expected. Remember that people came to America looking for freedom to choose their own lives and to pursue their happiness. And the laws of America say that all people are equal. Americans feel strongly that men and women are equal and need to share the work around the house. True, we are not happy about the fact that one in every two marriages ends in divorce. Divorce is extremely painful for both the husband and wife and is especially hard on the children. But we feel that the other choice—to live together in anger and unhappiness, to fight in front of the children—is much worse. Americans also feel that married partners must be faithful to each other. If my husband wants a girlfriend, he can do that, but he has to divorce me first (and vice versa). In many other countries, the man has many girlfriends and stays married to a very unhappy and angry wife. Many Americans don't get married until they are sure about their partners, so more than 10 million Americans live together before marriage. Some couples never marry because they want to keep their independence. And, in the gay community, many couples want to get married, but it's illegal in most states.

Most Americans believe that a good husband helps his wife in the kitchen. It is a wonderful chance for the couple to spend time with each other at the end of the busy work day, and it adds sharing and equality to the relationship. This is especially true now that many wives work outside the home. If both the husband and wife work outside the home, they both should do work in the home.

This equal sharing of responsibility is also true when it comes to raising children. Sometimes, if it's the wife who can make more money in her job, then the husband might stay home to take care of the children.

Try to find some American men, and ask them how they feel about these things. I think you will be surprised!

## P.S. (statistics from the U.S. Census of 2000)

✓ 2.2 million marriages take place in America each year. That's an average of 6,000 a day.

✓ The average age of a woman's first marriage is 25 years and for the man, 27.

✓ About 58 percent of Americans over the age of 18 are married.

✓ 92 million people (42 percent) of adult Americans are unmarried. Don't be surprised that this is often by choice.

✓ 51 million households (families)—44 percent of all households—are headed by unmarried men or women.

✓ 31 million (or 27 percent) of Americans live alone.

✓ More than 5 million unmarried partners of the opposite sex live together. That's more than 4 percent of all households.

# C. Children, Parents, and Pets

Dear Teacher,

*I just started work as a housekeeper for a very nice American family. They have two children, a boy who is 12 and a girl who is 14. The woman told me that I am not ever to clean up the children's rooms. Teacher, the rooms are so disorganized! The children throw their clothes and things on the floor, and they are supposed to make their own beds. The only thing she wants me to do is help them change their sheets once a week. The children seem nice, but I have never seen rooms like that. The mother and father are very neat, and they never allow the children to keep food in the rooms. When the children misbehave, instead of hitting them, they take away their cell phones or don't let them play with the computer. Is all of this normal?*

*Zenea*

———————————————

Dear Zenea,

I can understand your confusion, but American parents try to teach their children how to clean up their own rooms; the parents don't do it for them (and your employer doesn't want you to do it, either). Americans value accepting responsibility for their own actions. Parents try to teach their children, both boys and girls, to take care of their things at a very early age. Many parents insist that the children must keep the rest of the house neat, but they allow children to decide how to organize their own space. This gives the children a sense of personal freedom, an understanding of privacy, and an understanding that if their things get damaged because they are left on the floor, they will have to live with the consequences. Allowing children to learn how to be neat by themselves is a wonderful way to teach them independence and responsibility for their actions. Yes, Zenea, the majority of American children drive their parents crazy with "messy" rooms, but it's a great lesson for the children about how to grow up and become responsible adults.

As for punishment, in many states it is illegal to hit children (or anyone, for that matter), and so parents punish by taking away something that the child values. This teaches responsibility. Children learn early on that there are unpleasant results to bad behavior and that if they do something wrong, they will lose something they enjoy. This also (hopefully) gives children a message that they can control the outcome by not breaking the rules. Many Americans feel that hitting children just teaches them to fear their parents. It should be the child's decision to do what is expected or not. It sounds like you are working for a very normal American family!

---

*Dear Teacher,*

*American children are so different from children in my country. Even though they often carry teddy bears and dolls and torn blankets, they seem like little adults. In my country, children are treated like children and given a lot of candy. The children I see here ask a lot of questions and their parents talk to them like adults, giving them truthful answers. It seems like the children are always learning. Teacher, sometimes I'm embarrassed when I see parents from my country not controlling their children. For example, at the mall I watched a woman let her kids run around, playing and screaming in the shoe store yesterday. She did not stop her children, even though the saleswoman asked her to control them.*

*Alex*

Dear Alex,

Actually, it is a lot of hard work to be a good parent in the USA. We help our children learn to live with independence and freedom, and we teach them that freedom means responsibility. They need to learn this by experiencing it, not by what we say. We encourage them to ask "Why?" This helps them to better understand the world.

Many American parents begin to give children choices at a very early age. Slowly, the children learn that if they make the wrong choice, they will have to pay the consequences.

Americans talk to their children with respect, in an adult way, and try to explain everything to them, so that they can learn to think for themselves. We try to teach them the values of independence and respect for privacy, and to act toward others the way they would want others to act toward them. If the children do something wrong, we do not punish them by hitting but by taking something away that they value. If my child doesn't want to do her homework, that is her choice, but she can't watch TV.

It really takes about 18 years for our children to understand that freedom means responsibility. That time helps them become strong and smart enough to live on their own as responsible adults.

And you're right about the blankets and bears. Until children are five years old or so, they often carry around a *security blanket* (their old, torn baby blanket) or a stuffed (soft) toy. By the time they go to school, they don't need them any more. (Well, maybe only when they go to bed.)

*Dear Teacher,*

*Your country is so confusing. I'm shocked by how Americans are so crazy about pets. They treat them better than people! I have seen advertisements for "doggie" restaurants, hotels, boutiques, psychiatrists for troubled dogs, special food, and even special candles for dogs! To me, this is disgusting.*

*Also my co-worker was talking about his dog and he said, "She." I thought he was talking about his daughter! I was taught that we should use "it" for animals, but all the Americans I know talk about their pets with "he" or "she." This is very strange. The thing I don't understand is that I see so many homeless people in the street, looking through garbage cans for food. In my country, dogs and cats look through garbage cans for food, not people! I thought America was such a rich country. Why do I see many poor and homeless people and so many rich pets?*

*Danny*

---

Dear Danny,

Many Americans feel the way you do about the contrast between homelessness and pets. It is hard to explain why so many people are homeless or, worse, why the U.S. government doesn't have more programs to help them. The truth is that Americans love their pets a lot and often treat them like family. I guess it is just one place where Americans are completely comfortable showing their affection. Many people live alone in America and the dog or cat is often their only companion. In fact, 67 percent of pet owners (that includes adults) share a bed with their pets. There are more pets in America than people, and Americans spend more than $15 billion annually on their pets: food, toys, dog-walkers, medical services, pet funerals, and pet cemeteries.

Because most dogs in America are not working dogs (ones that work on farms or help the disabled or the police), Americans often think of their dogs as their children. So *he* or *she* are used to refer to pets because they are seen as almost human. I agree with you that it is disgusting to see dogs eat better than human beings, but loving and caring for a pet is common in American culture.

---

 ## P.S.

- ✓ American parents speak to their children as adults and teach them how to be responsible for their actions.
- ✓ American parents encourage their children to question and always ask "Why?"
- ✓ It is normal for American children to have very messy rooms.
- ✓ It is common for young American children to carry *security blankets* (their baby blanket) or a stuffed toy.
- ✓ Americans do not hit their children but discipline (teach) them by taking things away and explaining why and how the child could have done it better.
- ✓ Americans love their pets, sometimes more than they love people.
- ✓ There are 75 million pet dogs and 89 million pet cats in the United States.

# D. Senior Citizens

*Dear Teacher,*

*My co-worker seemed like a really nice person, but over lunch she told me some things that surprised me. First of all, she complained to me that her 20-year-old son dropped out of college and came back home to live with her. Teacher, she is charging him rent to live in his own mother's house! I lived with my parents while I went to college and after, too. In my country, no one would dream of charging their own family rent.*

*Then the next day she told me that her mother is very old and sick and she is going to make her mother move out of her apartment. (Teacher, her mother lives alone in an apartment!) My co-worker is looking for an "assisted living" apartment for her mother. Is that a hospital? If she were nice she would take care of her mother in her own home, because her mother took care of her when she was a child. In my country, we honor and respect our parents. We would never let them live alone or send them away when they got sick. I thought I liked my co-worker and we could be friends, but now I think very badly of her. Why is she doing these awful things?*

*SoonTre Lee*

———————————

Dear SoonTre Lee,

Let's talk a little about your co-worker's point of view. First of all, I'm going to guess that she is charging her 20-year-old son rent not because she needs or wants the money but because she wants him to go back to college. It is true that when the economy is bad, some American families do ask their children over 18 to pay some money for the mortgage or rent. Many Americans believe that once a child reaches the age of 18, he or she is an adult and needs to be, or learn to be, independent. (Sometimes the age is higher, like 21 or 22 depending on the situation.) You cannot learn to be independent if your parents treat you like a child or take care of you by paying for you. Americans value independence highly and expect their children to do things for themselves without depending on others. On the other hand, American parents who have the money will usually pay for their child's costs to attend college and housing for as long as it takes to get the chosen degree. But because your co-worker's son dropped out of college, he may not get any more financial support from his parents.

Most older Americans do not want to live with their adult children. Because Americans value independence so much, older Americans are extremely uncomfortable "being a burden" or using the money of adult children. They are also afraid to lose their freedom and independence when they move into their "child's" house. Your co-worker probably does love and respect her mother. She wants to give her the independence her mother needs to be happy.

*Assisted living* is a special place for older people who need help cooking and cleaning and taking care of themselves. They get the care they need there, but they still have some independence. Making the decision to put her mother in this place was probably very difficult for your co-worker. Talk to her some more and try to understand why she did these things. Ask her general questions like, "How is your son?" or "How is your mother doing?" Maybe you'll see that she is really the nice person you originally thought.

---

*Dear Teacher,*

*There is a student in my college English class. He is an American and his name is Marvin. Teacher, he is 78 years old! He said that he retired from his insurance business when he was 65 and then he became a real estate salesman. Now he wants to get a degree in journalism from the college. I have never heard of an older man doing such a thing. By the time he gets his degree he will be 80. Who will hire him? Is this normal?*

*Ruth*

---

Dear Ruth,

First, it's not polite to refer to Marvin as an older man. He probably feels quite young. He is normal. Most Americans retire only when they want to; there is no mandatory (forced by law) retirement age in the USA—that would be discrimination (unequal treatment). Those who love their jobs work until they can't do the job correctly. Others retire early so that they can do other things. It is not uncommon to see students in their 50s and 60s going to law school; many people in their 40s and 50s go to medical school or become teachers, nurses, etc. Many Americans go back to college to get second or third degrees. It is common for Americans to have two or three careers in their lives. We want to live life to the fullest and pursue our happiness. Become friends with Marvin. You might learn a lot from him.

# P.S.

- ✓ Older Americans value their freedom and independence and do not want to be taken care of by their families.
- ✓ The majority of older Americans prefer to live in *retirement homes* for independent living than to live with their grown children.
- ✓ Americans are living longer and are healthier, and many do not want to retire from their jobs.
- ✓ Those that choose to retire usually get another job, pursue a hobby, or go back to school.

## Caution

- ✓ Be careful. Try not to refer to people as "old" or "older." Even *senior citizens* want to feel young and independent.

# E. Homosexuality

*Dear Teacher,*

*I don't have a bath in my apartment, so I decided to go to the bath house. In my country, we all go to the bath house once a week to take a hot relaxing bath. But, Teacher, when I got there, all these men looked at me like I was on sale and they were trying to figure out if they wanted to buy me! I saw men kissing and doing other things I can't believe and cannot write about. I couldn't relax at all and left really quickly. Can I not take a bath in America until I buy a bathtub?*

*Also, I often see men holding hands with men and I've seen women kissing each other. What does this mean? Is this legal? How can it be allowed? This is not what we do in my country.*

*Ali*

---

Dear Ali,

I'm sorry you had such a confusing experience. Seeing open homosexuality can sometimes be shocking for foreign students. Let me explain a few things. The U.S. Constitution and the laws of America guarantee equal freedom of choice to all people. Most major cities in the U.S. are more accepting of homosexuality than other countries are. In most cities the word *bath house* means a place where gay (homosexual) men can go and meet each other and, if they choose, have sex. Most straight (heterosexual) men do not go to bath houses. If you want a relaxing experience, look up "spas" in the Yellow Pages or on the Internet. In some cities, especially on the West Coast, there are many Korean spas, which are similar to the bath houses you miss in your country.

Because homosexuality is accepted in most major cities, gay (men) or lesbian (women) couples are often comfortable showing affection to each other in public. However, in more conservative and rural areas, it can be dangerous for gays and lesbians to be open about their sexuality. Some parts of the USA are very accepting, but others are not. To answer your question, straight men do not hold hands with other straight men and straight women do not usually hold hands or kiss other women on the lips.

## P.S.

✓ Homosexuality is protected by law in the United States.
✓ 4,300,000 adult Americans or 1.5 percent of the population identify themselves as gay, lesbian, bi-sexual, or transgender.

# F. Domestic Violence

*Teacher,*

*I had a shocking experience yesterday. When I picked up my son at his pre-school, they wouldn't let me get him until a policeman talked to me. They wanted to know why my son had red marks on his arms and neck. Teacher! They asked me why I burned him with a cigarette! I explained that my mother has always had bad pains in her arms so I "coined" my son to protect him from the "bad wind" he might get from her. In my country, we always "coin" to protect our health. We heat a copper coin—I used a penny—and put oil on it and then rub it on the shoulders, back, chest, neck, or arms. The school made me sign some papers. A woman, they called her a "social worker," is coming to my house. Teacher, first of all, I would never hurt my child. Second of all, what business is it of theirs about my family? I feel so ashamed.*

*Nguyen*

---

Dear Nguyen,

I am sorry to hear about your experience. In America, where we generally practice Western medicine, most people don't know a lot about other kinds of medical practices. Obviously, the people at the pre-school didn't understand your tradition of *coining* and were very concerned by what looked like burn marks on your son. They thought it was a serious case of child abuse. In the United States, it is against the law to hit or physically hurt anyone, including using a belt to spank (to hit on the bottom) or a fist (a closed hand) to hit your child, spouse, parents, or even your pets. We call that *domestic violence*. It is a serious crime. Unlike many cultures, American law says that it is the responsibility of all the members of the society to protect all the people, not just a private family matter. In fact, Nguyen, at this school, I have to sign a statement each year that if I see any signs of domestic violence against or toward any of my students, I have to report it to the administration. Whenever we think there is a problem of domestic abuse with our neighbors or co-workers we do not get involved ourselves, but we do call the authorities to investigate. Just last week I heard my neighbors fighting with each other. The wife was screaming "Help!" so I called 911. I wasn't being nosy. I was just taking my responsibility as an American seriously. Even if it was okay in your country for a husband to hit his wife, it is not okay in the United States. The husband—or whoever is doing the hitting—can go to jail.

Nguyen, I suggest you go to google.com or ask.com and search for "Asian Coining." Print what it says and give it to your son's teachers, so they will understand that you are a loving and responsible parent.

## P.S.

✓ Domestic violence is against the law. It is illegal to hit anyone—a spouse, a parent, a child, or even your dog!

✓ If you (or someone you know) have a problem with domestic violence call the National Domestic Violence Hotline: 1-800-799-7233. It is free and private and you can talk to a counselor in almost any language. Or, you can call 911 and talk to the police.

✓ One million calls are made to the National Domestic Violence Hotline each year. For more information, go to www.ndvh.org/.

✓ Approximately 1.3 million women and 835,000 men are physically assaulted by an intimate (close) partner annually in the United States.

## Caution

✓ If your child has any bruises (red or blue marks on the skin) from a fall or *coining*, etc., explain to the teachers before they think that it is something worse!

# Celebrations and Gifts

# A. Weddings

Dear Teacher,

I had such a strange experience at my cousin's wedding. First, when my husband and I got there, we signed the guest book and asked where to put our money card and envelope. A young man pointed to a table full of gifts. I saw big boxes wrapped beautifully. There was even an ironing board with a bow on it! All I had was a special envelope with $100 cash. I didn't want to put it on the table with all the big presents. It could have gotten lost or stolen.

Then I looked at the other guests. I wanted to go home and change my clothes! In my country, when a woman is invited to a wedding, she puts a lot of time and preparation into the way she looks. We spend a lot of time choosing a beautiful dress, and we are very careful to match our shoes to our purse. If we don't have a nice dress, we buy one. We always make an appointment with the hairdresser for the day of the wedding and we wear our best jewelry.

My cousin was born in my country, but she grew up here and married an American who she met at college. This was my first American wedding, and I did everything I normally do for a wedding in my country. The only people who were very dressed up were my relatives, the bride's family, from our country. The people who weren't dressed up were the Americans from the groom's family and all of their friends. It was embarrassing for me and my relatives because the groom's family was wearing very simple clothes. Why do American people dress the same at a wedding as a picnic?

Teacher, the wedding was strange. My cousin and her groom were married by a woman! There were many parts of the ceremony I did not understand. It was so different from weddings in my country. My husband and I tried to have a good time, but now I know I have to learn much

*more about American culture and customs. That will help me enjoy being*
*here and maybe I will feel more comfortable.*

*Zoya*

---

Dear Zoya,

I am sure you and your relatives looked beautiful in your special clothes. Maybe the groom's family felt underdressed. American weddings are all very different. They can be casual and informal or formal. You can look for clues (helpful suggestions) on the invitation. If it says "black tie," it means men should wear tuxedos or very nice suits and women should wear formal dresses. Most weddings are just dressy. We wear the same clothes we would wear to an evening party. The style of the invitation and the time of day might give you an idea about how formal it is. Events that occur during the day are more casual. Evening events are more formal. Americans usually wear something nice to a wedding, but we don't want to wear something that draws too much attention to us because it should be the bride's day. Guests don't wear white because that color belongs to the bride. We would only wear a white dress if it has many other colors in it. Women often wear black, especially at evening weddings. Black is often a color of formal clothes. Men usually wear dark or black suits.

Most American couples *register* for gifts at a specific place—for example Target® or Macy's®. *To register* for gifts means that the couple chose what they want and made a list that the guests can look at, either at the store or online at the store's website. This way guests can buy what the couple wants so the couple doesn't get the same things. Some couples tell you on the invitation where they are registered or you ask someone else, like the bride's mother, or the maid of honor (the bride's closest friend or relative). In the past, it was tradition for American couples to receive presents like toasters, dishes, silverware, or towels. Now, because most couples are getting married at an older age, they already own these things. Although it is not an American tradition to give money, it is becoming more popular and common. Be sure you put the money in a card, and be sure to sign your name so the couple can thank you. Zoya, you were right to feel concerned about the cash. A check is always better than cash, in case the envelope gets lost.

There is no one style of American wedding. Most weddings are a combination of the bride's and groom's cultures and religions. Some weddings take place in a church or temple and have a reception after. Some weddings take place in someone's house, a public place like a park or the beach, or a museum or the zoo! Even though all weddings are different, they all have the same purpose: to bring two people, two families, and their friends together. You are right about learning about customs and cultures. The longer you're here, the easier it will be. I hope you have a good time at the next wedding you go to.

---

 ## P.S.

- ✓ American weddings are all very different. They can be casual or formal.
- ✓ Many American couples register (make a list) for gifts at specific stores.
- ✓ There is no one style of traditional American wedding. Most weddings are a mixture of the bride's and groom's cultures and religions.

# B. Birthdays and Anniversaries

Dear Teacher,

I don't know what to do about birthdays and anniversaries. I was invited to a co-worker's birthday Saturday afternoon. I don't know him very well, so I didn't know what to give him. My wife and I decided the best thing would be $30 and a cake. When we got to the party, and my wife gave his wife the cake, the wife looked confused. I watched when other people came in, and they brought beautifully wrapped boxes or wine. One person brought a salad.

Teacher, my wife and I were surprised at this American man's birthday party because it was a lot like a child's party. His wife put a cake in front of him with candles. We sang the birthday song, he blew out the candles, and then we all ate the cake. His wife put our cake out much later, but very few people even looked at it. My wife had spent two hours making it and decorating it. Also, there were a lot of signs that said, "Over the hill." I don't know what that means, Teacher, but it didn't seem very respectful.

We weren't sure what to do with our envelope, so we put it on the table with the other gifts. In our country, we don't open gifts in front of people, so we were surprised and embarrassed when my co-worker opened the envelope. He looked a little shocked when he saw the money. He smiled and said "thank you." I could tell from the other guests' reactions that we had done something wrong. Also, some of the other presents and cards seemed cheap and rude and disrespectful because they made jokes about his age. Next weekend, my wife and I are invited to an anniversary party for my wife's boss, and we don't want to make any more mistakes. What gift should we bring? Do we bring food?

David

Dear David,

Let me explain a little about American culture. Americans view age differently than other cultures. We do not honor age in the same way that other cultures do. Many Americans have mixed feelings about growing old, so people make jokes and celebrate birthdays in similar ways as we did as children. But they do this only for certain birthdays (like 40, 50, 60, 75). The expression *over the hill* means you are getting older (usually on your 40th or 50th birthday). You have climbed to the top of the hill in your life. Now, the future will be all downhill! This is a way of teasing (making fun of) someone while at the same time recognizing their age. I agree with you that some birthday cards and gifts seem rude, but most people think they're funny. I think it's just that Americans aren't comfortable with getting older, and so they joke about it instead.

It is an American tradition to open presents toward the end of the party after eating the cake. Guests often watch the birthday person open the gifts. Then the cards and gifts are looked at and passed around. People invited to birthday parties are expected to put some thought into their gifts, and they are rewarded by having their gifts publicly opened and appreciated. But not every adult chooses to celebrate in this way.

What to buy someone for his or her birthday or anniversary is a very difficult choice for most Americans. Some people are simply better at knowing what the other person wants than others. The best way to choose a gift is to think about the person and what he or she likes. You probably don't know your wife's boss that well. My advice is to get a gift card for a department store or a neighborhood store or restaurant. When you don't know what to buy someone, a gift card is a good idea because the person can get something he or she wants at the store you choose. It's like giving money, except that in this situation giving money is seen as not appropriate. People typically spend $20–25.

Because an anniversary is for two people, you might think about spending more, depending on how much you can afford. If you don't know any of your wife's boss's interests, you can always give a gift card to a nice restaurant to have a nice dinner. You'll find that the more practice you have giving gifts and writing cards, the easier it will become.

 **P.S.**

✓ Some Americans have mixed feelings about growing old.
✓ If a birthday party for an adult is held, Americans open presents and cards in front of people.
✓ When you don't know what to buy someone, a gift card for a store or restaurant is appropriate.

# C. Baby and Wedding Showers

Dear Teacher,

You said that sometimes we realize an important part of our culture only when we see something different. I didn't really understand what you meant until this weekend. I was invited to my co-worker's baby shower. My co-worker was pregnant and went on maternity leave (when the woman stops working because she will soon have a baby). I hadn't seen her for a few weeks. When I got the invitation, I saw the RSVP (call to say if you can come or not) you told us about. I followed your advice and called the telephone number and said, "Thank you, I can come." On the invitation it said she was registered at Target®, so I went there and got a present she had registered for. I got to the hostess's house exactly on time. Teacher, I felt so proud of myself.

I was so excited to see the new baby. But when I got there, there was no baby. My co-worker was still pregnant! Teacher, this is such bad luck in my country! Of course, I don't really believe what my grandmother told me about magic spells, but I actually felt sick. I had bought a gift for an unborn child! In my culture, this is like wishing bad luck on the baby. I tried to smile and be friendly, but I had to sit down. I think everyone could tell something was wrong because the hostess gave me water and asked if I was okay. I went into the bathroom and looked in the mirror. I tried to remind myself that I was in America and that many Americans do not believe in bad luck. I reminded myself that the customs are different here and that, obviously, they didn't think I was wishing bad luck on the baby. But, they already had my gift. When I left the bathroom, I saw the husband and some other men in the living room. There were men at a women's party! I tried my best to have a good time and smile and practice my English, but I left early. I hope I wasn't rude.

*A few days have passed, and I feel a little better. Teacher, I had to talk to you about this. I just can't believe Americans have a baby shower when the baby isn't born yet! Is this normal? Also in my country, men are never at baby showers. The party is only for women. Is it normal for men to be there?*

*Tala*

---

Dear Tala,

I'm sorry you had such a tough time. It sounds like you were actually in shock. Isn't it interesting how things you don't even know are such a deep part of your culture can affect you? In America, the vast majority of pregnant women are given a baby shower **before** the baby is born. If the parents are adopting, the shower is usually given after the parents have the baby at home.

Americans are probably less superstitious (believing something is lucky or unlucky because of a feeling or something not scientific) than other cultures, but pregnancy is one time where all humans are unsure and so are extra protective. Even many Americans are a little afraid of bad luck at those times. Traditionally, American women do not tell anyone they are pregnant until after the first trimester (first three months) when there is less chance of miscarriage (losing the baby). Whether this is superstition or just practicality is unclear. Baby showers are usually held four to eight weeks before the date the baby is supposed to be born. At this stage in the pregnancy, the baby would most likely survive when it is born. The reason we have baby showers before the baby is born is because Americans are very practical. The reason for having the baby shower is for the guests to *shower* the baby with presents. The parents need those things before the baby is born. If we wait until after the baby is born, the mother might not be feeling well and might have to wait for weeks or months to be *showered*. Then, the presents would not be as useful. Most Americans don't worry that buying things for an unborn baby will bring bad luck.

As for your second question, in the past, baby showers were attended by women only. Recently, men have taken a much more active role in parenting. Some couples say, *"we're pregnant."* Fathers share child care responsibilities much more than they did in the past. Baby showers are about babies, and it takes two to make a baby.

I hope this makes you feel better about your experience. I know you had a bad time, but now that a few weeks have passed, maybe you can think about it and compare cultures.

## P.S.

- ✓ There are two kinds of showers—bridal showers (for the woman before she gets married) and baby showers. Both of these were traditionally parties for women only, but they are both changing and now include men.

- ✓ Showers are supposed to be hosted by someone outside the person's close family. Although the idea is to give gifts, it's considered rude to have a family member have a party and ask for gifts for their relative.

- ✓ As with weddings, people register for gifts at a specific place. Find out where they are registered and get a gift early. The longer you wait, the fewer options you will have. Most people register for gifts that cost $10–$100 (or more).

- ✓ Diapers (paper) are almost always appreciated by new mothers.

- ✓ Be sure you include a card with your gift. The person being *showered* will want to send you a thank you card.

# D. Funerals

*Teacher:*

*My husband's co-worker's wife died. We were all so very sad. They loved each other very much and have two small children. But when we went to the funeral, we were shocked. There were yellow and red roses on the coffin. Not everyone wore black, and nobody made any loud crying noises. When some people got up to speak about her, they made some jokes and people laughed. There was no place to put money, and after the funeral we went to a party at someone's home. Is this normal?*

*Nouara*

Dear Nouara,

At a funeral, to show love and respect for the person who has died, Americans try hard to keep sad emotions deep inside. Of course, we cannot control our tears, but we try to control the noise. It is common not to hear sad sounds at an American funeral. Americans are very optimistic and even at such a sad time, we try not to think about the death but to celebrate the life of the person. As a result, we often try to remember and share happy memories and to laugh at those memories.

It often seems that the only time it is OK for Americans to lose control of their emotions in public is at a sports game or watching a game on television. You will hear Americans screaming in happiness or anger or disappointment, and all of this is very normal. Maybe that's why sports are so very popular and important in the USA.

As for yellow and red roses, why not? Maybe they were her favorite flowers and colors. We do not have the same deep symbolism of colors and flowers as in other cultures. Most people wear darker colors to a funeral, but it is not rude to wear other colors. There is no "death" color, and there is no "death" flower in America. Black is commonly worn to funerals, but it is considered a beautiful and elegant color and is often also worn to parties, weddings, and business meetings.

## P.S.

✓ It is not normal to make loud sad sounds at an American funeral. Americans try to keep strong emotions inside.

✓ There is no traditional color or flower that symbolizes death. Any and all flowers can be used at funerals.

✓ While the close relatives and friends of the one who has died usually wear dark colors, any dark clothing is accepted when you go to a funeral.

✓ Americans do not give money at a funeral. Sometimes we send flowers or plants to the ceremony. Usually we will give a donation to a charity in the name of the dead person. The charity sends a notice to the family.

✓ After the funeral, there is usually a reception at the home of the family. There is usually a lot of food and sometimes alcohol. The people talk a lot about their memories of the dead person.

✓ It is normal to send a sympathy card or a card that means "I am so sorry the person has died" to the family.

✓ In some religions, there is a *wake* or a *viewing* the night before the funeral, where you can say your personal good-bye to the dead person.

# Surviving in the City

# A. Public Transportation

*Dear Teacher,*

*I had such a terrible time on the bus this morning! First, I put a $20 bill in the machine and expected to get change, but the driver said I had to use "exact change." I didn't get any money back at all! He was very nice and gave me some transfers. Then I sat down in the front and people looked at me strangely. Then I saw the place I wanted to get off, but the bus didn't stop and I didn't know what to do. There was only the driver. In my country, there's always another person who collects the money and calls the bus to stop when we ask. I spent an hour on the bus because I didn't want to get off and get lost. At least in America, the bus always comes on time and follows the schedule, and the driver was nice and polite.*

*Gayane*

―――――――――

Dear Gayane,

Here are three things you need to know that will help you next time.

1. On most public transportation, you need to have the exact amount of money. The driver cannot make any change for you because he or she needs to worry about driving. Usually you don't pay the driver. You put your money into a machine next to the driver. If you take the bus or subway and don't have a bus pass or token (a special coin that is used like money for buses, toilets, etc.), be sure to always carry a lot of change with you—dollars and quarters and sometimes dimes.

2. The seats in the front of the bus are usually reserved for the elderly (old people), the disabled (people with physical problems), or pregnant women. Most people go toward the back of the bus. If the bus is very crowded, you can sit in the reserved seats as long as you immediately get up if someone who looks like he or she needs that seat gets on the bus.

3. In the United States, buses only stop at their bus stop, and they will stop only if there is someone waiting, or if one of the passengers signals that he or she wants to exit the bus **before** getting to the bus stop. This can be confusing the first time, so be sure to get a copy of a bus map or ask the driver. A few blocks **before** you come to your stop, pull the wire that hangs next to the windows, or press the button STOP REQUESTED. Be careful, and do not push the button marked EMERGENCY. These buttons are usually in the front and middle of the bus. This will signal the bus driver that someone wants to get off at the next stop. Also, in bigger cities, be careful when you take an *express bus*. Those buses don't stop at every stop, so tell the driver where you need to get off and ask him or her if the bus stops there.

---

*Teacher,*

*My wallet was stolen yesterday! I fell asleep on the bus and when I woke up, someone had cut the side of my purse and taken out my wallet. I had $400 in it and all my documents and a photo of my grandpa who died last year. I feel so very sad. I don't know what I can do!*

*Chi-Ching*

---

Chi-Ching, I am so sorry to hear these stories of pick-pockets (people who steal wallets and purses). Do not carry anything with you that cannot be easily replaced. Unless you need them at that specific time (except, of course, for your driver's license), try to only carry a photocopy of important documents. If you have documents that cannot be replaced, be sure to keep the originals in a safe place at home. If you must carry them, hide them somewhere on your body, like in a little bag under your clothes. You can often find these *hidden wallets* at travel stores or office supply stores.

As for money, many Americans rarely carry more than $50 in cash. They have credit cards and checks that can be replaced if lost or stolen. As you know, once cash is gone, it is gone. If you know you will be in a dangerous situation, carry a few dollars in a wallet in your pocket or purse and then keep the important papers, credit cards, or cash in a more hidden place (money belt, in your shoe, in the little bag around your waist or neck, etc.).

---

*Teacher:*

*Today, I was sitting on the bus when an older woman got on. I stood up to give her my seat, and she got angry with me and said she didn't need it. Did I do something wrong?*

*Boris*

---

Boris, you were being very polite, but the woman probably felt hurt because she doesn't want you to think she is old. She wants to keep her independence. If she needed a seat, she would have asked you to give it to her. Americans value independence and feeling young.

I recommend that you continue to be polite to people but understand their feelings and that they might want to keep their independence. Try using eye contact and body language first. If she had wanted the seat, she would have come over and nodded or said yes. Each person is an individual, and you need to make decisions depending on each unique situation, not their age or physical state.

Something else to remember is never push people in a wheelchair or physically guide a blind person without first asking them if they want help. Most disabled Americans are strongly independent and feel hurt and/or angry when people insist on helping them when they feel they can do it themselves.

---

 ## P.S.

✓ There are special seats in the front of buses for disabled people or senior citizens.

✓ Americans do not carry a lot of cash with them.

✓ Americans carry credit cards and checks.

✓ Protect your property by hiding money or important documents on your body or at home.

✓ Most buses require the exact amount of money and cannot give change back.

✓ Most buses have special stops, so you need to pull the cord or push the button to request the stop. They cannot pick you up or let you off anywhere you want.

## Caution

- ✓ Unless he or she asks for it, giving your seat on the bus to an older or a disabled person might cause him or her to be angry. Most older (or disabled) people do not want to be thought of as needing help.
- ✓ Watch out for people who want to steal your wallet or purse.
- ✓ Allow passengers to get off the bus before you get on.

# B. Walking in the City

Teacher,

In my country, there are so many cars in a hurry that it is hard to get across the street. We just go when we can. Yesterday when I was running across the street, the policeman stopped me and gave me a ticket for "jaywalking." What does that mean? What did I do wrong? Do I have to pay it?

Ki Beom

In most states of the USA, the one who walks (the pedestrian) always has the right of way. In the United States, drivers must always stop at a red light, and they must check the crosswalk for pedestrians. But sometimes, unfortunately, drivers are drunk, talking on the cell phone, text messaging, or changing their CDs so they are not paying attention. When the light tells you it's okay to walk, always be sure to look both ways to check that the drivers are paying attention. When there is no signal light but there are white lines painted on the street at the intersection (the white lines are called the *crosswalk* where the pedestrian has permission to cross the street), the law in most states is that the minute the pedestrian steps off the curb (the little "step" between the sidewalk and the street), the cars must stop. But, again, remember to be careful. Some cars might not stop or they might not see you. If you run across the street in traffic, *and not in a crosswalk*, the cars are not expecting you to be there. They might not see you so you could be hit. It is really only safe for you to cross at the crosswalk with the green light or at an "unmarked" intersection (where two streets cross but there are no white lines on the street) because the cars are expecting you only there.

*Jaywalking* means crossing the street when it is not at a marked crosswalk or intersection, or when the light is no longer green. In most states you can get a jaywalking ticket if the red hand or other symbol tells you there is not enough time to get safely across the street. Some signals show you how many seconds you have left.

Ki Beom, pay the ticket, and be happy that you have learned a lesson that could save your life. If you don't pay the ticket, they could charge you even more money and if you have a lot of unpaid tickets, they could send you to jail. If you visit San Francisco, Chicago, New York, or other crowded cities like that, you might see a lot of people running across the street in the middle of traffic. They usually don't get tickets, but they could, and most of all it's very dangerous. Waiting a few minutes for the green light could give you a lifetime of extra minutes!

**P.S.**

- ✓ Pedestrians always have the right of way (but cars are bigger and stronger!).
- ✓ Pedestrians must cross at a crosswalk or at an unmarked intersection; crossing in the middle of the road is called *jaywalking,* and it is against the law.
- ✓ If crossing at a stoplight, pedestrians can only cross when the pedestrian light is green; when it says stop, you must not begin to cross.
- ✓ Do not run when you cross the street; the driver cannot correctly judge where to stop the car.

# C. Driving in the City

*Teacher,*

*I just got my driver's license. I studied the laws, and it took me three times, but I finally passed the written test. It took me three more times to pass the driving test. (I just can't parallel park very well!) Yesterday I was on the highway, and everyone was going so fast. The car in back of me kept blinking his lights and honking his horn at me. He made me so nervous that I got off the highway. Why was he so rude?*

*Ludmilla*

---

Dear Ludmilla,

Driving in a new country can be very difficult. Some drivers are in more of a hurry than other drivers. It sounds like you were probably going too slowly, which can sometimes be as dangerous as going too fast. Or, you were going too slow for him! While you're improving your driving skills, I recommend that you stay in the lane on the far right. This lane is slower. The cars don't go as fast as the cars in the first and second lanes do. Sometimes cars go faster than the speed limit, and you don't want to get hit, but you also don't want to speed and break the law. I can tell you that the more experience you have driving, the more confident you'll feel. Keep driving. Be sure to understand the directions before you go somewhere. Give yourself plenty of time to get to where you want to go. Don't talk on your cell phone while driving. Every time you park your car on the street, be very sure to check all the signs for the parking hours. Also be sure to check if there are parking meters (little machines you put coins into, like renting the space). Some cities don't have parking meters, but they have a special machine in the middle of each block where you buy a permit. Often you need to put the permit or notice on the window of your car. Follow the instructions on the machine.

---

 ## P.S.

✓ Obey all traffic laws when driving.

✓ Always wear your seatbelt. In most states, it's the law. In all states, it's common sense.

✓ Remember that walkers always have the right of way.

✓ Although it may be legal in your state to talk on your cell phone while driving, it is not a good idea unless it is an emergency. In that case, pull to the side of the road.

✓ Get directions to your destination before you go, and read them two or three times before driving.

✓ Be aware of laws about children and car safety. In most states, children must sit in a special seat and in the back seat until a certain age. In some cities, adults cannot smoke in a car where there are children.

✓ Always check the parking signs for hours, street cleaning, tow away (the police will take away your car), etc.

✓ Remember driving is not a race or a game. Be calm and polite at all times.

# D. The Police

*Dear Teacher,*

*I'm sorry I was absent yesterday, but as I was driving to school a policeman made me stop the car. I saw him in my mirror and thought I was doing everything right. He seemed so mean when I opened my car door to get out. He said, "Sit back down" in a loud, angry voice. He told me to show him my license and registration and insurance. Fortunately, I had them. I tried to show respect, but he really frightened me. He told me my left brake light was out and sat in his car a long time. Then he gave me a ticket. Of course I fixed the light this morning. Do I have to pay the ticket? Should I have given him some money? I didn't do anything wrong. I was so upset I couldn't come to class.*

*Dario*

---

Dear Dario,

Remember that police are sometimes killed when they stop someone, so they can be nervous. In America, if we are stopped by the police, we stay in the car. We roll down the window and keep our hands on the steering wheel (to show that we do not have a gun). We smile at the officer and look him or her directly in the eyes. We say, "What seems to be the problem, Officer?" Dario, you probably showed respect by not smiling and not looking him in the eyes. That probably made him think you were doing something bad. Americans do not trust people when they cannot see their eyes. He then sat in his car to check your license on his computer. This is always done.

It is a bad idea to argue with the police. If you think that the police are being unfair, you can argue your case in court. The best thing you could have done, while smiling, was to say, "I didn't know my light was out. Thank you, Officer, for telling me. I will fix it immediately." If you did that, it is possible that he wouldn't have given you the ticket, but not definite.

The ticket you had was not a serious *moving violation* and may not have a fine. Look at the instructions on the ticket. You probably will have to go to some office so they can check the car to see that you fixed the light. If you just ignore the ticket, you will have to pay a penalty and you could go to jail.

Dario, I am so glad you did not give the policeman any money. He could have arrested you. In the USA, it is a crime to try to bribe, to pay money to someone so you can get something from them, like the police. As a matter of fact, it is a crime to try to bribe anyone—a secretary, a city worker, or a teacher. Unlike many countries, we never pay the ticket directly to the police officer. We either mail the money as a check or money order—but never cash—in the ticket's envelope, or go to court to pay.

# P.S.

- ✓ If the police put the lights on to tell you to stop your car, move to the side of the road right away.
- ✓ Stay in your car.
- ✓ Put your hands on the steering wheel.
- ✓ Roll down the window.
- ✓ Look directly at the officer and make eye contact.
- ✓ Smile.
- ✓ Say, "What seems to be the problem, Officer?"
- ✓ Do not argue (the officer is right, anyway).
- ✓ When you drive, be sure to always have your license, registration, and proof of insurance with you.
- ✓ Say thank you to the officer.
- ✓ Never, for any reason, give money to the officer. Tickets are paid through the mail or in court. Giving money to the police or any public employee is called a *bribe*, and it is a serious crime in the USA.

# E. City Services

Teacher,
*There was a dead cat in front of my house. It had flies all over it and was smelling really bad. I called 911. The operator was really rude and said it wasn't her problem and hung up. What did I do wrong?*

*Yousef*

---

Dear Yousef,
When you dial the police, fire or ambulance emergency number 911, it is only to report an emergency of life or death (of a person). Unfortunately, we do not have enough police or operators to handle non-emergency services. When you move to a new place, it's a good idea to check with your city council representative (or alderman), your public library, your neighbor, a teacher, or a friend to find out what public service numbers are used in your city. Most cities use 911 for life and death emergency calls and 411 for telephone number information. Some cities now use 311 or 211 to deal with other problems like this. You would call and say "dead animal" and someone would connect you with the proper service. You can call your city representative or the library and get a telephone list of city services before you need them. Then, if you need to report a big couch in front of your apartment, a street light that is not working, or a big hole in the street, etc., you can talk to the right person. By the way, what happened to the cat?

## P.S.

✓ If it is not a life or death emergency, do not call 911. If you need to talk to the police or fire department, call your local police or fire station. You should keep these numbers near your phone.

✓ For information about your city, call your city council representative, use the Internet or phone book, call 411, or try the reference desk at your local library.

✓ Find out if your city has 311 or 211 information services.

# F. Tenant/Landlord Rights

*Dear Teacher,*

*I'm sorry I wasn't able to come to class for the last week. I had some serious problems with my landlord. The water in my kitchen sink would not go down. He said I had to pay to fix it. He said he would give me a plumber's number and that I needed to call and have the plumber come and then pay for it myself. I have only lived there for two months. I didn't put anything except water and soap down the sink. I didn't know what to do. Then I remembered the housing website you gave us in class last month. I couldn't really understand everything it said, so I followed your advice and called the number. You were right. I waited on the phone for about 15 minutes. Because you told me that could happen, I was prepared to wait. Finally, I talked to the woman on the phone. She was very nice and she said that it was my landlord's responsibility to get the plumber and to fix the problem. She also told me that if there were any other problems to call back and that someone who comes to check the problems (an inspector) would come to my apartment.*

*I told my landlord what the woman said, and he got really mad. He said that I didn't know anything because I wasn't an American. He said those rules were not for me! I got really upset. Part of me thought he was right, but then I remembered what you taught us about consumer rights and rights for everyone in America. So I got mad. I called the housing department back and an inspector came out. He told my landlord that if he didn't fix the sink immediately, he would have to pay a fine. Obviously now, my landlord and I are not happy with each other, but he knows he has to obey the law. I think he thought that because I am a foreign woman and I have only been here for a little while, he could take advantage of me. If it weren't for you, Teacher, he would have been right! Thank you so much for giving us that lesson and the website for the housing department. I feel so proud of myself because I've never been strong for myself like that before.*

*Mika*

---

Dear Mika,

Thank you for your letter. I'm so glad I was able to help you, and I am really proud of how strong you were. I'm also glad I got your letter because now I will make a point of teaching all my classes about their housing rights and giving all my students the website addresses.

Remember how I said that every state has different housing laws? Every state has rights protecting the tenant (renter) and explaining the rights and responsibilities of the landlord (owner). In the future, if you forget the details about your different rights, just go to the Internet. Using a search engine like google.com or yahoo.com, type "housing rights" or "housing department" and the name of your city.

In Los Angeles, the website is in Armenian, Chinese, Farsi, Khmer, Korean, Russian, Spanish, and English. In many other cities, it is only in English and Spanish or another second language of the city. Most websites have a phone number that you can call as well, but you may have to wait for a long time. You can always go in person to the office. Usually talking to a human is easier than trying to read the information. Most websites also have information on how to find a place to live. I'm so proud of you, Mika. Keep fighting for your rights.

*Dear Teacher,*

*You were telling us that in this city tenants have strong legal rights. My landlady is really bad. I wonder if I should report her. First of all, she charged me $50 extra because I paid my rent a little late. She said it was my responsibility, not hers, to get rid of the cockroaches. What do you think?*

*Caesar*

---

Dear Caesar,

Did you sign a rental agreement or a lease when you moved in? It probably explained the normal policy of late rent. I am sorry to tell you that your landlady probably has every right to charge a late rent fee, usually 5 percent of the rent. Caesar, that is fair. Your landlady has payments to the bank for the loan on her apartment building and property taxes, insurance payments, and water and power bills to pay on time. When you don't pay your rent on time, she will be late paying her bills.

As for cockroaches, the laws of this city say that if the apartment was clean and free of cockroaches when you moved in, then you are responsible for removing the cockroaches that came after you moved in. Don't spray any poison. It might work for one day, but the roaches will come back. Go to the store and buy those "roach motels" (little boxes of cockroach poison), and put them under your kitchen sink, under your refrigerator, and in the bathroom. Change them every three months. Caesar, I'm sorry, but cockroaches love our city. The weather is great and they live here, happily, all year round. You can't make them go away forever, but you can keep them under control.

## P.S.

✓ Check with your city council to find out the tenant/landlord laws of your city and state. You can sometimes find the information by searching online. Type in the words "tenant laws" and the name of your city, or check with the reference librarian at your library.

✓ Rent must be paid on time or there is usually a late fee.

✓ If you don't pay your rent, the landlord has the right to go to court to get permission to evict you (have you and your property removed).

✓ If you pay your rent by check, be sure you have enough money in your bank account. If your check bounces (there is not enough money), you will have to pay extra money, between $10 and $50.

✓ If you pay by cash, be sure to get a receipt.

✓ In almost all states and cities, the tenant has the right to demand an apartment that is safe and healthy. If you don't like the color of the walls or carpet, that is your problem.

# G. Strange Laws

*Teacher,*
*I met some new friends and we went to a sports bar to see the World Cup soccer game. There was a really big guy standing at the door who asked for my ID. When he saw my age (I'm 20), he wouldn't let me in! I told him I don't drink alcohol. I just wanted to see the game with my friends. But he wouldn't let me in. I was so embarrassed.*

*Vladimir*

---

Dear Vladimir,

We have some strange laws in America. You join the Armed Forces (Army, Navy, Marines, National Guard, etc.) and fight and die for your country at age 18. You can make important choices and vote in elections at age 18. But you cannot buy alcohol, drink it, or be in a place where alcohol is served until you are age 21. Places will ask for your ID until you look like you are older than 30! Don't even think of going to Las Vegas, casinos, or other places to gamble if you are under the age of 21. It is illegal to buy cigarettes if you are under age 18. In most cities and states, it is against the law for anyone, no matter what age, to drink alcohol in any public place like on the street, in a park, at the beach, etc. You can only drink alcohol in specific restaurants, clubs, and bars, and, of course, in your home. In some cities, and in some states, it is against the law to buy or sell alcohol on Sundays.

## P.S.

✓ You must be over the age of 21 and have some photo identification to buy or drink alcohol.

✓ In most cities and states, you can only smoke in specific places; in many cities, you can only smoke in your own home—not in restaurants, bars, hospitals, places of work, parks, etc.

✓ In most states, it is illegal to buy cigarettes if you are under the age of 18.

# H. Garage Sales

*Dear Teacher,*

*My wife bought a blanket at a sale in someone's yard. Someone had died, and her daughter was selling a lot of the things in the house. My wife said it was a really nice blanket, very clean, and only three dollars. I think it's disgusting to buy other people's things. We would never do that in my country. We only buy new things. The only people who buy used things are very poor. To buy something from a stranger who has died is asking for bad luck. But my wife really likes going to these sales. Is it safe for her to go? Is it safe for her to buy things that come from strangers?*

*Kenji*

Dear Kenji,

These kinds of sales are extremely popular in the USA. They have several names: garage sales (often to clean out a garage), yard sales (selling used things in the front yard), rummage sales (usually at a church or school to raise money), or estate sales (if someone has died). There are also moving sales and divorce sales. Americans always hope to pay less money for something, so they love these kinds of sales. You can buy nice things for a very low price. This is also one of the few times that you can try to bargain for or get a lower price in the United States.

Generally speaking, it is safe to buy books, clothes, furniture, baby clothes, dishes, and glasses at garage sales because you can see if they are in good condition or not. Be more careful with electronic equipment, cameras, or computers.

Many people who have sales just want to throw away their things to make room for new things (but they also want to make some money).

Anyone can have a sale. Some people advertise in newspapers, and some people just put up signs on the street corners. Use your judgment; trust your feelings when you talk with strangers. Be careful with what you buy. It might be better to buy some items at a store. You (or your wife) can decide what you feel comfortable with. What you find at sales can be a good way to get something new (to you) and save money.

Also, unlike most countries, the best way to bargain in America is not to criticize what you want to buy. Don't say, "This old thing is torn and dirty." Instead say, "I really like it, but I can only spend $2 ($5, etc.). Could you lower the price a little?"

Try it, Kenji. Go with your wife to a sale or two, and find out what you can learn about American culture from the things people are selling. Happy shopping!

---

 **P.S.**

✓ You can also shop for bargains at thrift stores like the Salvation Army or the Goodwill Store.

✓ You might find bargains on Craig's List on the Internet (just go to <u>craigslist.com</u>, find your city, and go to "Things for Sale"). There is a free section; you just have to go to the place and take away what is offered.

**Caution**

- ✓ At a garage sale, it is not recommended to go into a stranger's house or a basement alone.
- ✓ Be cautious buying any electrical item like a computer, television, camera, small oven, or iron unless you can test them for more than half an hour.
- ✓ You cannot return anything at a garage sale. Everything is sold "as is."

# The Workplace

A. Job Interviews

B. Unwanted Attention

# A. Job Interviews

*Teacher,*

*Next week both my wife and I have job interviews on Wednesday. We have no idea what we should wear or how to act. Please help.*

*Mansour*

---

Dear Mansour,

There are so many different fashions and styles now that it is difficult to say exactly what is appropriate (correct) to wear. I always recommend that you wear more formal clothes when you are not sure.

You always want to be clean and neat. Be careful that neither of you wear too much aftershave or perfume. Your wife (and you, for that matter) should keep the jewelry to a minimum. Don't wear hats!

If the job is professional, a suit is always a good idea. You can wear a dark suit or dark pants and a nice jacket with a white or blue shirt. Often a tie is not necessary, but it is usually a good idea to wear one. Your wife should wear either a skirt suit or pantsuit in darker colors, or a nice dress. Tell her to wear nice shoes but not high heels. She should keep her make-up to a minimum. She can wear lipstick (not bright red) and mascara, but no dark eye shadow or heavy eye-liner. Of course, I don't need to tell you both not to smoke or chew gum.

If the job requires you to work with your hands, like a cook, housekeeper, or gardener, then dress a little more informally. If you or your wife wear a suit, the employer might think you will feel too good for the job. A clean white shirt or t-shirt and jeans for you, and a nice, simple dress or skirt/pants and blouse for your wife with very little jewelry for the both of you would be fine.

You also asked me what is the best way to act. Don't forget to be there on time. Being a little early is even better. Remember that Americans think that "time is money"—both time and money are valuable. If you are late to the interview, the employer will think that you will be late for work. Try doing a *test drive* on Tuesday to see where the offices are. Check the traffic and the parking so that you will not be late on Wednesday.

It doesn't matter if you are a man or a woman, at an interview both you and your wife should act the same way. When you meet the interviewer, be sure to shake the interviewer's hand firmly. Be sure to look the interviewer in the eyes, and be sure to smile. Answer the interview questions in a positive and honest manner. Be careful not to talk too much. I know that it may be very hard to speak positively about yourself, but it is extremely important. I know it will be hard for your wife to say good things about herself because it does not come naturally in your culture. You will be asked about your *assets* (good qualities), and you must describe what they are. Tell the interviewer that you are responsible and reliable. Say that you come early and leave late. If he or she asks you about any negative qualities, just say that you take your job too seriously. Be sure to thank the interviewer for the opportunity, and don't ask about sick days or vacations until they have offered you the job. It's often nice to send a thank you letter or email after the interview, but keep it short and make no writing mistakes. I would be happy to check it for you.

Be sure to review your resume (the one-page paper that lists your job experience and education) so that you can correctly answer questions about dates and names of previous jobs. You might want to review the lessons we had on job interviews.

---

## P.S.

✓ Be sure to dress appropriately for the job interview.

✓ Be on time!

✓ Be sure to say positive things about yourself. Do not feel embarrassed when you do that. Speak strongly and not softly.

✓ Smile and look the interviewer in the eye.

✓ When the interviewer says, "Do you have any questions?" thank him or her for the opportunity to have the interview. Don't ask about sick days or vacations at that time.

# B. Unwanted Attention

*Dear Teacher,*

*I work as a bookkeeper in a small accounting office and I love my job. It is close to my home, and my work schedule lets me come to school as well. The manager is making me really uncomfortable. For the past few months, he has often come very close to me when I am working at my desk. He stares at me and smiles and winks at me (closes one eye quickly and keeps the other eye open) and puts his hand on my shoulder. He is always telling me how pretty I am and comments on my clothes. I tried to ignore it, but yesterday he invited me to dinner at his house. Of course I said no. Today he told me that he was thinking of promoting me and wanted to discuss it at dinner next Friday night. I really don't want to go to his house, but a promotion at a better salary would be so helpful. What do you think I should do?*

*Anjelika*

---

Dear Anjelika,

This sounds like a serious case of employment discrimination (unequal treatment), a kind of discrimination that is called *sexual harassment* in America. He is bothering you because you are an attractive woman. This is absolutely against the law. Unfortunately, sexual harassment is very hard to prove, and it's even harder to get justice. I just read an article that said that 40–60 percent of working women have been sexually harassed (and men get harassed by their employers, too).

If your business has more than 15 employees, you are protected by the federal EEOC (Equal Employment Opportunity Commission), and you can file a complaint (see information on the website www.eeoc.gov). If your company has fewer than 15 employees, you might be protected by state laws so you can file a complaint with the state agency that deals with sexual harassment. Go to the state website.

The first thing to do, of course, is to say, "No!" Do not go to your manager's house. Say it politely at first. If he gets angry, then be stronger. Is there someone at the office you can talk to? Do you have a human resource person (personnel director) there? Is there a supervisor you can talk to? Be sure to keep a record and write about everything the man says and does, with the date and time. It would be great if you had witnesses (people who have actually seen the problem).

In reality, you are in a very unpleasant situation. Although sexual harassment is against the law, it often happens that you, the victim, will not be happy at your job. The manager obviously has more power than you. I know you want to keep the job, but if it doesn't get better, you might have to consider finding another place to work. Good luck and tell me what happens.

 ## P.S.

- ✓ *Sexual harassment* is considered employment discrimination. It is against the law and is considered a serious crime.
- ✓ If you are being sexually harassed, talk to someone at work.
- ✓ File a complaint with your state or with the federal EEOC.
- ✓ 40–60 percent of working women have been sexually harassed (and men get harassed too).

# Schools

# A. Taking Tests and Cheating

*Dear Teacher,*

*Yesterday's test was horrible and unfair. The reading comprehension test had 25 questions, and you gave us only 35 minutes. When you said the time was over, I only had half of the test finished. I don't think it was fair when you took the paper away from me like you did.*

*Xavier*

---

Dear Xavier,

I'm sorry that you feel unhappy about the test. Remember when I told the class that taking a test was just like playing a game? You need to have some ability, but mostly you need to know how to play by the rules. The rules for soccer are not the same for football, and the rules of American tests are not the same as in your country. Most American tests are timed (just like football and basketball) and when the timer rings, the test is over (the game has ended). That means all pencils must immediately be put down on the desk. Remember, I told you to read the questions *first*, looking for the key words, and then to hunt for the answers in the reading selection. I told you not to spend more than a minute and a half on each question. Because we aren't using a computer, I told you that you didn't have to go in order, but you should do the easy ones first and to guess if you weren't sure. That's how we play the test game. Xavier. Next time you will do better, and in America, we grade on improvement.

*Dear Teacher,*

*I had a terrible experience last semester. It was my first time in an American college. I was very happy and a little nervous coming to school. First, I was so surprised that students can wear whatever they want to school. It was so very different from my country. When the teacher gave me an assignment to write a composition, I began to copy from my classmate. Suddenly, my teacher saw what I was doing, and she made me leave the room. She gave me an F on the assignment! I was so embarrassed I went home and cried.*

*The next week, I was taking a test in class and my friend asked for help. I tried to help her, but the teacher got very angry at me and took away both our papers. He said that we would both get F's on the test because we were cheating. I was only trying to help! I didn't have a copy of the answers. What did I do wrong?*

*Lilit*

---

Dear Lilit,

In America, "helping" someone on a test is considered cheating. In the U.S., we value individual work. It is extremely important that you do all the work by yourself. If you studied and your friend didn't, why should she get the credit that belongs to you? When you take a test in American schools, you cannot use a dictionary (unless the teacher says you can). You cannot talk to anyone about anything, look at any papers that have the answers, or look at anyone else's test paper or "help" your friends. If you have a question about what to do on the test, you are expected to raise your hand and let the teacher come to you. You should not get up and leave your seat until you are finished. If you help someone cheat, you will be punished along with the cheater. If you want to help your friend, help her study before the test.

In most universities, plagiarizing a paper (using someone else's work or copying from a book or copying information online and saying it's your own) can get you expelled (removed) from the university. Be proud of your work and don't cheat. We teach our children that when they cheat, they are only hurting themselves. The knowledge you learn in school is more important than the grade you get on a test. By the way, if you do badly on a test, you can always take it again and again, until you get the score you need. If you are caught cheating, it is possible that you may never get a second chance.

## P.S.

- ✓ Tests in America are timed. Watch the clock.
- ✓ Spend an equal amount of time on each question.
- ✓ Work as quickly as you can. If you finish early, go back and check your answers. Don't just get up and leave if you finish and there is time.
- ✓ On most tests, it is OK to guess; in fact, it is expected. If points will be subtracted for a wrong answer, the test directions will tell you.
- ✓ Do the easy questions first.
- ✓ If you have a problem or a question, immediately ask the teacher for help.

## Caution

- ✓ When taking a test, do not look at your neighbor's paper.
- ✓ When taking a test, don't let your neighbor look at your paper.
- ✓ When taking a test, do not say anything to anybody.
- ✓ When the test is over, immediately put your pencil down.
- ✓ Don't even think of cheating! If you don't do well on a test, you can probably take it again and again until you get the score you need. If you are caught cheating, you probably will not get another chance.
- ✓ Do your own work. Copying from a book, a friend, or the Internet is called plagiarism, and it is considered very bad. You could get removed from school or fired from a job if you plagiarize.

# B. Teacher Expectations and Student Responsibilities

*Dear Teacher,*

*I don't understand why I got a C in your class. I came every day and did all the work. To show respect, I never looked directly at you when I talked. Unlike the other students in the class who were always talking, I was quiet. There were several students who were very rude, asking you questions all the time and even disagreeing with you. I don't understand why they got A's. I don't mean to be disrespectful, Teacher, but I want to get an A next semester. What can I do to get this grade?*

*Myung Duk*

Dear Myung Duk,

I'm sorry you're upset with your grade, and I'll be glad to explain it to you. I tried to tell you throughout the semester that you needed to speak more in the class. The students you describe as rude were actually the best students. Maybe in other countries, students are expected to just sit quietly in class and listen, but in the USA, we value people who think for themselves. In America, a good student is one who always asks questions. The students who had their own opinions were not rude to me, they were just trying to better understand what we were studying. You will learn much more if you think about it for yourself than if the teacher just gives you the answer. I now realize that you kept your eyes down to be respectful, but in America, to show respect, you must look people in the eyes. If you don't look someone in the eyes, that person will think you have done something wrong or you are not interested in them. Myung Duk, you are a good student, but you must ask questions, and talk to your classmates. If you always do your homework, study for tests, ask questions, and come visit me during office hours when you have special questions, you will probably get an A next semester.

## P.S.

✓ Students should ask questions all the time. Raise your hand straight up in the air. Do not make any noise. When you are recognized, put your hand down. There may be a stupid answer, but there is never a stupid question. Never feel embarrassed about making mistakes.

✓ If you come to class late, just come in the door. Do not say anything. Just sit down. Saying "Good morning" or "I'm sorry" or standing by the door is considered rude in the USA. It disturbs the rest of the class!

✓ When you enter the room, remove your hat. Wearing any kind of hat indoors (except for religious reasons) is considered extremely rude in the USA. Also, remove your dark glasses. Americans need to see your eyes to be able to trust you.

✓ Do not put on make-up or nail polish in the classroom. Do not wear so much perfume or aftershave that your neighbor can smell it. Be sure to use deodorant. In America, any strong smells are considered rude because you are taking away your neighbor's right to his or her personal space.

- ✓ Do not chew gum in the class. If you have gum in your mouth, throw it away correctly. Put all gum that has already been chewed in paper. Throw the paper in the trash. Do not stick it under the desk.
- ✓ Turn off all cell phones. It is rude and disturbs the class.
- ✓ Always call your teacher by his or her name. Teachers will usually tell you what they want to be called. It is important to use someone's name (Mrs. Smith, Mr. Smith, Professor Smith), not just a job title (Teacher), to show that he or she is an individual.
- ✓ In many countries, students must wear uniforms. In the U.S., uniforms are rare.
- ✓ In all U.S. schools, it is illegal for teachers to hit students. Also, teachers must never embarrass students or make them feel ashamed.
- ✓ You can almost always find free adult education. In the U.S., it is never too late to go back to school, even if you are 80 years old!
- ✓ Children from the age of 6 to 16 must attend school in the United States. Each state has its own laws before age 6 and after age 16.
- ✓ If you have a personal problem, ask to talk to your teacher after class, or go to his or her *office hours*.
- ✓ It is permitted (and a good idea) to visit most college and university campuses. Walk around to see what they are like. Visit the cafeteria, the bookstore, and the buildings. If you see a very large lecture class in session, just sit in the back for a while and listen.

# Health and Personal Matters

# A. Staying Clean and Healthy

*Teacher,*

*Yesterday, I found a note on my desk at work and nobody signed it. Teacher, the note said that I smelled bad and the note was held by a rubber band around a bottle of deodorant. I am a very clean person, Teacher, and I use body spray everyday and wash my hair every other day. Isn't this terribly rude?*

*Ana*

---

Dear Ana,

I'm sorry that you got that anonymous (unsigned) note. Of course it hurt you. But you need to understand that Americans try to be really careful about not bothering anyone else with their own personal body odor (smell). Most Americans take at least one bath or shower each day and always put on a good underarm deodorant after their showers. They wash or clean their clothing the minute they suspect there might be any kind of smell on it. (Body odor on clothes cannot be hidden with perfume.) Americans also wash their hair at least once a week, often every day. They brush their teeth at least twice a day and often chew or spray *breath fresheners* in their mouths.

Ana, I'm sure you have noticed all the deodorant and mouthwash commercials on TV. When you go to the drug store, you will be amazed by the many deodorants for men and women and the number of toothpastes and breath fresheners for sale. You might think Americans are a little crazy with this subject, but it is hard for us to know if we have a strong body odor because it is ours and we are used to it. We consider wearing strong perfume or having strong body odor rude because it invades (goes into) someone else's personal space.

If your co-worker felt that there was a problem, he or she should have just spoken to you in a nice way. Talking about personal things like body odor is very embarrassing for both people. I understand why the note was unsigned. By the way, showering every day and using body sprays doesn't solve the problem. Only using deodorant and constantly checking your clothing works. Try the deodorant and see if you notice a difference.

---

## P.S.

- ✓ Americans are really careful about not bothering anyone else with their body odor or bad breath.
- ✓ Most Americans take at least one bath or shower each day and always put on a good underarm deodorant after bathing.
- ✓ Most Americans wash or clean their clothes after wearing them one or two times.

# B. Talking to a Doctor

*Teacher, my son had an ear infection and was crying and crying. We went to the emergency hospital and, Teacher, they made us wait for eight hours! He cried the whole time, and then they told us we had to pay $450 plus pay for the medicine. Is this normal?*

*Hilaire*

---

Hilaire,

I hope that your son is fine now. Unfortunately, many of my students tell me the same story. You sit and sit in an emergency room for hours and then you are charged a high fee. But, Hilaire, that is because in America, the emergency rooms of hospitals are supposed to be only used for life-or-death emergencies. Your son was sick and unhappy, but they had to take the patients with heart attacks or accidents first. In the USA, you are expected to have your own personal doctor, and when you or your family are sick you are supposed to call that doctor. If it is truly an emergency, the doctor will call the hospital and tell them you are coming. Unfortunately, it is now a very difficult economic time in the USA. Although 84 percent of the population (245 million Americans) have some sort of health insurance, many people do not have any form of medical insurance. Because not everyone can pay their medical bills, it raises the cost of doctors and hospitals for everyone.

The best thing to do is to ask some family or friends if they like their doctor and then go meet that doctor before you or your family get sick. The next best thing is to find a neighborhood Urgent Care clinic. Be careful because sometimes they are very expensive and sometimes the doctors are not licensed.

Remember, hospital emergency rooms are only for life or death emergencies. At the present time, they are often very busy and expensive.

---

*Dear Teacher,*

*I'm confused about my doctor's advice. I've been feeling sick for a long time, and I've had a lot of headaches. My doctor told me to take aspirin every day to feel better. I did that, but my headaches continued and now my stomach hurts. I saw him two weeks ago, and he told me that I was fine. He said that I was just imagining the pain. I asked him if I could have migraines (extremely bad headaches) or a sinus infection (an infection in the nose). I also said I was worried I might have brain cancer. He said he would give me a prescription for migraine medicine and that I couldn't possibly have brain cancer. He told me that I was wasting his time. I've been taking that migraine medication for two weeks, but I still have headaches, and they are getting worse and worse. I need to make another appointment to see him, but I'm afraid he will just tell me I'm wasting his time again. I feel really sick and scared. What should I do?*

*Estrella*

---

Dear Estrella,

I am so sorry that you feel so sick. Now I understand why you have been absent so much. My first piece of advice for you is to find a new doctor. Doctors are only human and can make mistakes, but it sounds like your doctor doesn't care or understand. A good doctor listens to the patient. Remember, it is your body, and you (or hopefully your insurance) are paying for his services. No doctor should ever tell you that you are imagining pain. It is extremely important that you trust and respect your doctor. It is also important that you feel that your doctor listens to you. Remember, Americans demand choices, so even if you are with an insurance company, you should be able to change your doctor. Also, whenever you have a problem where one doctor can't help you, you should ask to see a specialist. Estrella, you need to see a doctor who specializes in headaches. You have the right to ask for a *second opinion*. You have the right to not have to wait for a few weeks. When it comes to your health, you really need to fight for what you need. No one knows your body, your symptoms (the different signs of your sickness), or your pain better than you do. Doctors can give advice, but they don't always know what is best for you. Good luck, Estrella, and let me know what happens.

---

 ## P.S.

✓ If you have any questions about your medical treatment, get a second opinion. You must remember that when a doctor recommends a certain treatment or surgery, you will feel some pain because of the treatment or surgery. You will feel the pain, and you will pay the bill.

✓ If you take care of a medical problem when it first starts, you may save your life. If you suspect something is really wrong, get it taken care of immediately. Waiting might make it worse. Not getting something checked because you are afraid or don't have insurance might be seriously dangerous in the future.

✓ You can always ask the receptionist how much it will cost for the doctor's appointment. If you have insurance, you will probably have a *co-pay* (a certain amount you pay each time you see the doctor). If the doctor sends you to see a specialist or get a test, ask if it's covered by your insurance.

✓ If you don't have insurance, ask if the doctor's office gives a discount for uninsured patients (some places give you 10 percent off).

✓ When you need to make an appointment with a doctor, list all of your symptoms in English before you call. That way you will feel comfortable with the English words, and you won't forget anything important. If you have Medicare, an HMO, or private insurance, bring that information with you when you make the call and visit the office.

✓ Most states have free or low-cost clinics. If you need to see a doctor about a problem that is **not an emergency, do not go to the emergency room.** Most clinics have both *walk-in* (first come, first served) and appointment hours. It is best to make an appointment ahead of time; then you won't have to wait as long as if you just walk in. But do expect to wait; bring a book or your English homework.

# C. Using Bathrooms

*Teacher,*

*This is so embarrassing, but I don't know who else to ask. It's about toilets. My friends and I went to a nice seafood restaurant on the beach. I needed to find a toilet, but the two doors had words I didn't understand. One door had "Gulls" with a picture of a bird, and the other had "Buoys" with a picture of a big ball in the water. Teacher, I didn't know what to do. Lucky me, a man came out of the one marked Buoys, so I went into the one marked Gulls. But then, Teacher, when I sat on the toilet, it suddenly flushed (the water emptied) all by itself and scared me. Then two other women came in to use the toilets and they were talking to each other the whole time. Is all this normal?*

*Paola*

———————————

Dear Paola,

These embarrassing experiences are hard to talk about but are important. Every culture has different sizes, shapes, and styles of bathrooms and many different ways of using them. It is often difficult and embarrassing for a foreign adult to understand the mysteries of the American bathroom/restroom system!

Unlike most other countries, America rarely has public toilets available for everyone to use on the streets or in the subways. However, public restrooms can be found in most department stores, supermarkets, restaurants, cafes, gas stations, libraries, public buildings, etc. Now, because of the high number of homeless people, it is getting harder and harder to find an easy-to-use public restroom in the buildings of larger cities. Often, the bathrooms are locked and the customer must ask for the key. In most places, there are usually two different doors to different rooms with toilets inside—one for men and the other for women. (Of course, parents can take their little children into the one the parent will use.) They are often marked with a stick figure and/or labeled MEN and WOMEN. They might be called *restrooms, bathrooms, toilets, Mr. and Mrs., ladies and gentlemen, boys and girls, powder room* (for women), *washroom, lavatory,* etc. In large restaurants and public places, the bathrooms often have many toilets available, all separated by walls for privacy. Those are called *stalls.* The men's room usually also has a *urinal* without private walls. In smaller stores and restaurants, there might be only one bathroom, to be used by everyone (but one at a time).

Sometimes, in restaurants (like the one you were at, Paola), they try to be funny. For example, you were at a restaurant near the beach. *Gulls* is the name of a big white and grey sea bird, and it sounds like *girls.* A *buoy* is a large ball in the ocean that measures distances, and the word sounds like *boys.* A few years ago a German student of mine had a similar problem to yours. She was at a Texas-style steak restaurant. The toilets were labeled *His'n* and *Her'n.* That really meant *His* and *Hers.* But, in German, the man's bathroom says *Herren* (men), and so of course she didn't go in the door marked *Her'n.* She went into the one marked *His'n.* She quickly left when she saw a man inside.

Paola, when you are not sure, ask someone or wait and check to see who goes in or comes out.

All restrooms should be clean. Usually they have a special paper to cover the seat and toilet paper. Unlike some countries, most plumbing in America can accept toilet paper and seat covers and, for health and safety, both kinds of those used papers must be flushed down the toilet and never thrown away in a trash can or on the floor. In the women's restrooms, there is often a special little *sanitary* can on the wall or on the floor near the toilet. That is not for the toilet paper but for women's special needs (used tampons or pads). There should be a sink with hot water, soap, and paper towels, which go in the trash can. Sometimes, there is a hot air hand dryer instead of paper towels. Some restrooms have little machines that sell emergency products, perfumes, condoms, special supplies for women, etc.

To stay healthy, after using the toilet, always be sure to wash your hands with warm water and soap. If the toilet is not clean and/or there is no soap or paper, tell the manager.

Unlike toilets in some other countries, the toilets in America are designed to be sat on. When people stand on them, the seats break.

Recently, to save water and help the environment, toilets and sinks have become automatic. Those toilets flush (empty) by themselves. That can be quite a surprise if you are not expecting it. Often you can see a little red light behind the automatic toilet, and sometimes, if the toilet does not flush, push that button and the toilet should flush. With automatic sinks, you often need to move your hands under the faucet (what the water comes out of). Rarely, you might need to push on a pedal on the floor beneath the sink to start the water.

To ask where the bathroom is, you should ask, "Excuse me, where is the restroom?" It is strange, I know, but many Americans will go into a bathroom with a friend and continue their conversation at the urinal or in the next stall. It is common for Americans to talk on their cell phones while using the bathroom, and yet most adult Americans feel very uncomfortable talking about what they have been doing in the restroom.

I hope this helps you with some of the mysteries of bathrooms in America. Thank you for your trust.